Mom at Last

Mom at Last

How I Never Gave Up on Becoming a Mother

Sharon Simons

NEW YORK

Mom at Last
How I Never Gave Up on Becoming a Mother

ISBN 978-1-61448-442-4 paperback
ISBN 978-1-61448-443-1 eBook
Library of Congress Control Number: 2012952889

Morgan James Publishing
The Entrepreneurial Publisher
5 Penn Plaza, 23rd Floor,
New York City, New York 10001
(212) 655-5470 office • (516) 908-4496 fax
www.MorganJamesPublishing.com

Cover photograph taken by:
Jen Campbell of
Jennifer Seay Photography

Cover Design by:
Chris Treccani
www.3dogdesign.net

Interior Design by:
Bonnie Bushman
bonnie@caboodlegraphics.com

In an effort to support local communities, raise awareness and funds, Morgan James Publishing donates a percentage of all book sales for the life of each book to Habitat for Humanity Peninsula and Greater Williamsburg.

Get involved today, visit
www.MorganJamesBuilds.com.

Habitat for Humanity
Peninsula and
Greater Williamsburg
Building Partner

I dedicate this book to my loving husband Rick who was willing to take a second chance at fatherhood and strapped on his seatbelt along my bumpy road to motherhood which eventually brought us across the globe to Russia.

Without him I wouldn't have the two best gifts in the world. I am so thankful for my children Dylan and Hunter and thankful for the gift of adoption.

Table of Contents

Chapter One

The Baby House

··

The baby house hasn't seen new paint in decades. That's
what they call it, the baby house. Where they keep all the
abandoned Russian babies. More precisely, it's where the
state agency keeps all the unwanted Siberian babies, or maybe just
the Novokuznetsk babies, the small town we have driven hours to
reach. The baby house is concrete block covered in dirty stucco and
the facade has a slightly depressing rhythm to it: stucco and window
and patches of exposed concrete repeated in long horizontal bands
across the front of the building. It doesn't look anything like a house
for babies, wanted or otherwise.

The air inside our car is heavy and smells of cigarettes, sausage, and
mayonnaise. We sit there at the edge of a dirt parking lot for a long
moment and stare out the window. By "we" I mean my husband, Rick,
and me in the back seat, and in the front, our interpreter in her punkish
ball cap and a bulky Russian driver. Outside, the sky is not entirely gray-
blue, but strangely the same gray-blue of the baby house. As I sit here
staring out the window, what strikes me, other than the bleakness of the
place, is that there isn't a baby, a child, or a wayward teen in sight.

What little I know of orphanages I learned from my father. My recollection of my father's childhood runs through my mind as we approach the baby house for the first time.

My father didn't tell me his life story all at once. So I had to get it piecemeal over many years and some of the pieces remain missing. All I have are his cobwebby tales, snippets, sometimes just a sentence I can cut and paste into another story he told me years earlier.

My father's father was in the merchant marines and thus rarely home. At age five my father's mother died and a neighbor took him and his sisters in while his father was out at sea. His father soon remarried.

The new wife, my father's stepmother, was an evil witch, to hear Dad tell it when he's in the mood to say anything at all about his upbringing. When I dig deeper, he usually shuts up. But when he does let fly with some unexpected chunk of memory, I hold my tongue and listen. I am always amazed how he fills the dead air with more of his story, even when he really doesn't want to.

My father was dumped in an orphanage at nine and was let loose at sixteen. These are my words not his.

I remember a night many years ago when my father and I were sitting in his living room, he in his recliner, me sinking into a comfortable sofa. He spoke slowly in a low voice, possibly to keep my mother from overhearing. He said that as a kid he used to wet the bed and each time it happened, his new mother had taken to tying him to the old red maple in the backyard. After he told me, he turned to face me, paused for a long moment as if thinking how and what to say next, and said, "All I remember is hand-sized orange and yellow leaves. I'd look up into the tree and see all those leaves just days from falling down on me."

I told him there are now rules about tying children to trees.

"That woman wouldn't have followed no rules," my father said.

My father put up with this grouchy stepmother and absent father for four years. That was when his father died of a "terrible" accident, meaning no one would tell him exactly what happened. The stepmom promptly hauled the three kids over to St. Mary's Orphanage in Newark,

New Jersey, and left them inside the redbrick building. Saint Mary's Orphanage anchored the corner of South Orange and Sanford Avenues and looked to a frightened nine-year-old more like a prison than a devoted home for orphans. The orphanage was run by fifteen or so Catholic nuns, each seemed meaner than jailhouse guards and as uncompromising as cold steel.

Orphans like my father and his sisters ate week-old stale food and were glad to have it. For all his years at Saint Mary's, what my father remembers the most is being hungry. And fearful. This took place in the 1950s where discipline was revered, especially in orphanages, and included smacking the children with wooden paddles to enforce obedience.

Most years, during the holidays, people bearing gifts for the children visited the orphanage. On each such delivery event, the nuns would smile and pat the backs of well-meaning businessmen, lawyers, and church leaders doing their good deed for the year. The nuns would mumble as if praying, say thank you, wave, and shut the doors. They then would have several of the stronger boys stack all the gifts in a large room, used mostly when the nuns wanted to hide things from the children, and that would be the last anyone would see of the presents.

While my father was in his early teens, he would hustle up odd jobs in town delivering newspapers and fixing broken fences and anything he could do to earn a few dollars. He would hide the money in his room where often a greedy nun would snatch up the cash and disappear. Regardless, during his time there my father always endeavored to act correctly, study hard, and better himself.

Future moms and dads would occasionally arrive at St. Mary's ready to adopt a child and my father would dress, slick back his hair and stand in line with all the others awaiting inspection. For seven years, he endured these examinations. But despite his efforts to look good, model behavior, and burning desire to leave Saint Mary's, he was never chosen.

The happy ending to this story is that his older sister, also a St. Mary's orphan alum, escaped, married at seventeen, and marched right back to Stanford Avenue and pounded on the big front doors until someone handed over her little brother. Which they did.

But it's time to enter the baby house and see our real flesh and blood boys for the first time.

"This is it," Rick says. "Here we go."

I look at him and smile because that's what I do, a woman who hankers for the bright side of things, the good and the positive. If I have to, I'm perfectly willing to put on blinders and blot out all the ugliness in the world, if it helps me get what I want. And right now I want inside the baby house.

I reach for the door handle and this little gesture sets everyone in motion. We crawl out of the minivan and I take a deep breath and grip the two little brown teddy bears we brought with us. Rick holds a bag of baby clothing and a few other items and hustles us inside. The lobby of the baby house is a spiritless dump, describing it as "cozy" or even "welcoming," would be a blatant lie. Again, no babies. I learn later that we are not allowed to see any of the other orphans and thus they are hidden conveniently out of sight. I want nothing so much as to hold my baby boys, precious little Siberian tikes I have only glimpsed in photos thirty-five days ago. In one photo Dmitry is dressed in a pink jumpsuit and he stares up at the camera, frowning, his mouth slightly open, ready to say something quirky or maybe angry. Sergey is dressed in a black and yellow bumblebee outfit, arms in the air, and he has this loving, needy look in his eye.

My husband, Rick, is a cardiologist and cardiologists are compulsively alert to looming problems. He spent I don't know how many years at Penn State and then medical school and then in his practice looking inside the body's dark corridors for impending problems. Before we agreed to make the trip, he reminded me what we might be in for. "A lot of fathers and mothers of Russian orphans are alcoholics," he told me. "Vodka," he said using his doctor's voice, in a way that was both stern and caring. "They can't keep a job and they can't raise a baby, so they drop the child off at the baby house. Only the child has fetal alcohol syndrome and nobody knows it." This was a month ago, and I can still see him making a little check mark in the air with his finger listing off troubles to come. Extreme difficulty forming social connections. Check. Trouble with emotional ties. Check. Zero impulse control. Check. Learning disabilities. Check. Check. Check.

"You're signing us up for a lot," he said, "if we take in a fetal alcohol child."

Nothing in any the documents we've received says anything about fetal alcohol syndrome or any other disease. Far from it. Every bit of information has given off a calibrated, but incomplete report of the boys, which probably explains Rick's skepticism.

"The boy's aren't sick," I said.

"I'm just saying."

"Do you want to reconsider?"

Here my husband softened, as he always did when we talked about the boys. "No."

"I'll love them no matter what," he said.

"Me too."

The director of the baby house spies us standing sheepishly in the lobby, trying not to touch anything. She marches out of her office and half-shouts something in Russian at us. Our interpreter, a skinny girl with glasses and her cap now tucked away, mumbles something to me I don't catch. I want to see the boys and I'm tired of being in the car, of meeting strangers without understanding the language, and tired of the way the Russian adoption process doles out cryptic, often conflicting, bits of information in small doses.

The director is blonde, round-faced and babbles on relentlessly. She has graying teeth and heavy makeup and a body several sizes too big for her clothes. Finally, she stops talking and stares at me, then at my husband, smiles and lets loose a little gruff noise. The interpreter says there is a small problem. They only have us down for one baby. She says it as if we'd stopped at a McDonald's and the bored sixteen-year-old at the window had forgotten to include one of our milkshakes.

"What do you mean?" I ask.

"The paperwork. It says just one," she says.

"Two," I say. "We've been over all this. The paperwork, the money, it's all correct."

The way it works here, way out in the boonies of Siberia, is if you want a baby, or two, you follow the rules. And here are the rules. You pay thousands up front to people in America, some whom you've never met, don't know, and don't fully trust. Then, once you arrive in Moscow, you take 10,000 dollars in cash and you put 5,000 in one envelope and seal the envelope. You take 4,000 and put it in another envelope. Seal it. You take the remaining thousand and slip it into a third envelope. At some point on your trek from Moscow to the baby house, a man will ask for one of the envelopes. You give him the envelope. No talking. No questions. Later, at another time and another location, another man will ask for another envelope. You give him the envelope. Same with the last envelope. For two babies, you double the money and the envelopes. No discounts.

What's the money for, you ask?

No questions. We already told you.

To what degree that money filters down to care for the babies isn't clear, but it's not much, judging by the dilapidated condition of the baby house.

The director and our interpreter whisper in Russian. Occasionally, our interpreter turns to me and says, "Is much better, I think." Or, she says, "Okay, the paperwork, it must not be correct." Or she says other things equally unlikely to get us anywhere. By now, I'm gyrating with unhappiness, straining to smile at the director, moving my hands and shaking my head, and beginning to feel what mothers must feel who have inexplicably lost a child. I haven't been a mother for even one second, and I have lost my child. This is a child I've never seen in the flesh, never held, never comforted, but the feeling of loss is no less real.

The director shouts and the interpreter says, "You get Sergey," and pauses and says, "now."

"Yes, of course I want Sergey, but I also want Dmitry." Here I pull out a photo, the one of Dmitry in pink, as if proving he is mine. I have his picture, don't I?

"Is not a problem," the interpreter says.

"Can I help?" I say knowing full well that I am ill-equipped to track down the whereabouts of a twenty-one-month-old in a far off Siberian baby house, especially if he is not so much lost as hidden.

"Is not necessary," she says. "The director, she is looking," which isn't true because the director is flashing her graying teeth at me, shaking her head as if to say, "Only one baby today."

Rick quietly intones something to me and the interpreter and the director whisper, but no one is looking for Dmitry.

Our interpreter nudges Rick and me down the hall into another room, this one radiant in its cleanliness and color and aura of hope, all elements conspicuously missing from the rest of the baby house. Without warning a thick-bodied woman appears with Sergey and carries him to the center of a little play area filled with toys and places him on the floor, the floor itself a flimsy ancient carpet that looks much like a giant board game, one that involves trains, train tracks, train stations and the like. Sergey is sitting squarely in the middle of the tracks but doesn't notice, or if he does, he appears happy to find himself at the center of things. The director casts a frown at us. We have an hour with him and we'd better get to it while she tracks down Dmitry, or at least that's what she means if not exactly what she says. I sit on the carpet next to Sergey, a fourteen-month-old cutie in his red-and-white striped outfit, and I brush his blond hair with my hand and glance from Rick to the interpreter to the backside of the director marching away, hopefully toward my other boy.

Sergey sits next to me, inhaling giant breaths through his nose as if breathing me in. I speak to him and make soft little cooing noises. Rick kneels beside us and takes Sergey's arm and strokes it. I show him the teddy bear, wriggle it to get his attention, and then I place it in his lap and let go. Sergey watches me, ignoring the bear at first, then leans his little head forward and smells it and wraps a skinny arm around its body and squeezes and squeezes.

There is more whispering off in the hallway and Dmitry finally appears, a tiny body cradled in a woman's hefty arms. Compared to Sergey, Dmitry is a mess. Our order for two babies has apparently gotten waylaid, and as a rush job Dmitry hasn't been properly prepared. He looks as if he's been plucked from a box of mischievous babies, shaken and lightly dusted like you might a blouse you hadn't worn in a while, and handed over. He isn't dirty exactly, but he isn't as spruced up and prepped as Sergey, as if the kids are only buffed, polished, and put on display when the adoptive parents show up for a test drive. He has red bumps all over his face from what I hope is only spiteful mosquitoes and nothing more serious. The bites, if that's what they are, have been treated with something blue and pasty dabbed over the red. My little Dmitry is polka-dotted in baby blue and rose-red and, given his sallow skin, the combination isn't at all pretty.

That, and he is wailing in one long, noisy, burst of anger, pain, or I don't know what.

Everyone vanishes. It's just Sergey and Dmitry and Rick and me off in one corner of the play area, our little family parked on the floor of a baby house in Novokuznetsk staring at each other. I hand Dmitry his stuffed bear. He takes the bear and holds it to his chest and wails. I speak to him, lift him, and rock his tiny body while pressing him to me. Still wailing, I pass him to Rick who stands and walks him and the bear in a circle in and around the toy motorcycle and the bright orange cones and the swing set. Dmitry doesn't even attempt to stop crying.

"This is normal, right?" I ask my doctor husband.

"It's not fetal alcohol syndrome, if that's what you're asking."

"That's not what I'm asking."

"I think he's freaked out," he says, "and why wouldn't he be?"

"You're not just saying that?"

"He's almost two years old. He's grown up in an institution. We're strangers. He doesn't know what's going on."

"Here, trade me. Take Sergey," I say. "I need a little alone time with this one."

Rick lifts Sergey and I reach up and hand Sergey his bear, but he's too small to get a good grip or he's not especially interested or life is okay with or without a stuffed bear from FAO Schwarz. He lets it drop to the floor.

With only ten fading minutes left in the hour, Dmitry's sobs subside. We gently place him on the floor. He reaches for a wooden block and squeezes it and raises his hand as if to throw the block and then thinks better of it and holds it between his pink legs. He crawls around and gathers up more blocks, pushing them ahead of him. The motion of little Dmitry moving off on his own and gathering up the blocks and piling them next to a banana-yellow truck, as he's likely been instructed, and then one by one gently placing each block in the bed of the truck, is so endearing I begin to tear up. I know he's smart. Stubborn, but smart. The sort who grows up to be an engineer, a neurologist, or an FBI agent.

Adopting a Russian baby is about as dependable as handing over a pile of money to a snake charmer. You might get a good show for your money. Or, you might get bit. The adoption might happen or it might not. If you think otherwise, you're kidding yourself. Even as I sit here on the floor of the baby house I'm scared silly that if I take my eyes off the boys, my boys, they might vanish. I have crazy and admittedly paranoid thoughts that Sergey and Dmitry might be stolen from me or carted off by wolves and spirited away into the backwoods of northern Eurasia.

And I'm not exactly sure of baby house protocol. Is it up to us to place dibs on the boys? Or is this some sort of parental test? Are Rick and I being graded? Is it up to the director to decide if we get one or both boys? Or none? Whatever the process, I want the boys.

With seven minutes to go, our interpreter returns with one of the big-armed caretakers and the director. The three stand at one end of the long room next to the toy gym, chatting in low tones and watching us. I glance up occasionally. I somehow want to prove that we can make this work, that Rick and I are the perfect father and mother for Sergey and

Dmitry, that we are divinely matched for the job, though how I plan to get this across is much less clear.

When our hour is up, a caretaker scoops up both boys, one in each arm, and marches down the hall. I hear Dmitry's familiar wail fading away. By now I've gotten used to it and feel as if he is shouting something important to me only it's in Russian and once I teach him to wail in English, we'll all be better off. I hear a door slam and that's that.

The director smiles, tugs on the hem of her red sweater, which only makes her pot-bellied tummy more conspicuous and turns and retreats into her office. She shuts the door.

Our interpreter says, "She says to come back tomorrow."

I don't speak, but stare down the hallway after my boys.

"The director, she says to bring diapers, other items as you see fit." When I don't respond, she says, "One more day." I have no idea what this means.

This is all part of the plan. We are on step eighty-seven out of, well, no one ever really tells you how many steps are involved. Never, during this entire process are you fully, comprehensively filled in on the details. And in hindsight, even if you were, it wouldn't do any good, wouldn't make you feel one bit better about the process or more certain about the outcome. The baby adopting process is shrouded in mystery and there's a pervasive element of suspicion and seediness to it, as if the whole thing is orchestrated by some underworld organization secretly supported by the Russian Federation. It's not, of course. But it feels that way. What you get is a snippet of information. And later another snippet. Or you might get three or four snippets of information at once. Beyond that you get a lot of wide-eyed and vague reassurances about what will follow. Most of it isn't a lie, but neither is it factually truthful.

The way this works: we visit the orphanage, visit again, sign some paperwork, and then leave the boys and return home for weeks, months, who knows, where life is considerably cleaner and there's a whole lot less confusion. We twiddle our thumbs while some anonymous bureaucrat sifts through our application, schedules a court date, then we fly back and go before a Russian judge.

Imagine you're me. The saddest thing you've done in years is abandon your babies in a dreadful Siberian orphanage. Yet that's exactly what you do. On the drive back to the hotel, you think about Sergey, how he looked a little anemic, flimsy in a way, but then you recall the way he glanced up at you with those ample peepers and you pick him up, and it's clear this little boy needed parents big time. And Dmitry with those powerful lungs screeching. You know he is surely saying something with all that volume and it isn't his fault his new mom can't intuit his meaning. None of that matters. What matters, you tell yourself, is that you have fallen in love.

But I'm getting way, way ahead of myself.

Chapter Two

Kissing My Last Frog

P aul is tall and handsome in a way meant to appear effortless, a man who, not three minutes into our first date, spies a small modish picture frame from across his living room as if he'd forgotten it ever existed, crosses the room, reverently lifts and presses the frame to his heart, then tenderly places the frame into my cupped hands, which is kind of icky and charming at the same time. I look down and see a slimmer, less-muscled version of the man in front of me standing in cap and gown on the steps of USC's Bovard Administration Building grinning the dopey grin of a college grad. He is a man who wears three-hundred-dollar handmade jeans—put together using an esoteric process of thirteen washings with hand dyeing between each washing to add depth. I'm told—a man who refuses to drive or even ride in, if he can help it, anything but a black Mercedes-Benz S500, which he refers to as the S-Class, as in "Leave yours out by the curb, we'll take the S-Class to dinner," and who describes himself as being in "the food business." Later while squinting at the label of a five-hundred-dollar bottle of Haut Brion in our waiter's pink hand, he throws in, "Oh, I also own some warehouses." My new beau forgets to mention he's also a con man or a pathological liar. Or both.

He never owned warehouses nor worked in the food business. He never graduated from USC, nor possibly ever attended, though he had once ambled across campus in cap and gown, which must have been awkward, snapping pics of himself, or likely asking a slightly naïve freshman to lend a hand, posing in front of recognizable buildings of red brick laid in a Dutch bond.

Paul and I first meet in October.

New Jersey, 2004.

He's so handsome it scares me.

I'm thirty-eight, a month away from turning thirty-nine. Way too close to forty.

It's not all my fault, which is my way of explaining that a handful of seemingly unconnected things conspired against me. Collectively, they blinded me to what now seems as obvious as a black swan in a bubble bath making shrill trumpet-like noises. I'm seconds from turning forty, or so it feels, and my genetic tick-tock is ticking away, making loud clanking noises meant to remind me that I'm not getting any younger. The noise is so pervasive, at least to me, that when I do see signs that things aren't as they appear, I ignore them. I want this, I say to myself. I want a man who cares about me. Someone who treats me like a jewel, who spoils me, sends me flowers and swears his entire day is spent thinking of me. And I want a man who wants to make a baby. Or two. Pronto. Before my tick-tock stops. Is that too much to ask?

I think Paul might be the One.

I mean it. Some days, I am positively, categorically convinced he's the one. The one who takes care of you in old age. The one who whisks you off to romantic getaways in New Hampshire where the two of you stumble on an inn and spa and get a room overlooking the bay and lounge in old rocking chairs on the balcony and eat breakfast in bed and sign up for the birch blanket wrap that leaves your skin tingling with the scent of eucalyptus and peppermint for days. That One.

For two months things were wonderful and I thought our relationship could be special. But on a cold Saturday night in December, Paul invites me to dinner at an upscale restaurant with a stunning view of the Navesink River. When I arrive at his home, he is standing at the ready by his car, the S-Class (imagine me raising both hands and making little bent-finger quote gestures). I lean into him and laugh, reach around his waist and give him a squeeze. He squeezes back but at the same time turns his hip into me and sort of bumps me, putting some space between us. He reaches for the door handle.

Something is wrong.

"What?" I say.

"What yourself?" he says. "Climb in."

Paul drives too fast and talks too little, which isn't like him. He jerks the wheel hard left and right to miss a blue VW backing out of a driveway. "Geez," I say and look at Paul, who doesn't look back, comment, or console me in anyway. We pull in behind a slow-moving work truck hauling chopped wood. Paul tightens his grip on the leather steering wheel and glares at the wood stacked neatly in the bed of the truck. When we arrive at the restaurant, mercifully ending an unpleasant ten-minute drive, I'm convinced if only at a subliminal level, that something's out of place. I tell myself that with a single clearheaded clue I can track this thing to its root.

Some little something doesn't add up and I have a bad feeling we are gliding merrily into a spat and later a loud squabble, most likely about the time our waiter serves up a petite filet or a plate of spicy gulf shrimp. If nothing stops us we'll move headfirst into a dinner-ending yell fest. We have yet to have an actual yell fest, but for days I've felt one coming on.

Paul has changed, shifted and repositioned himself as someone I know and I don't know at the same time.

Off to my right is the entrance to the restaurant. We wait in the car for the valet kid to appear. Paul is only half listening to me. He's hungry or angry at the missing valet kid or thinking about crashing into little blue cars or possibly he's replaying some bothersome happenstance at work—arguing with a client in the food industry (imagine those little bent "quote" fingers again) while strolling through one of his warehouses. Whatever it is, he's in a mood. He's all movement, hands and feet and head pulling in six different ways at once. The hands are busy rubbing down the wood grain dashboard with an organic cotton towel.

"I'm almost afraid to ask," I say.

"Ask," Paul says.

"You're sure?"

"Ask."

"You won't get mad?"

"Ask already."

"I drove by your office in the last few days. Several times. I have yet to see your car out front."

He examines the cotton towel for any signs of dirt. "That's a question?"

"That was the set up," I say. "Ready for the question?"

"Can we talk about this later, like after the kid parks the car? Maybe after we order a bottle of wine. What are you having for dinner, have you decided?"

"You're changing the subject."

"Am I?"

"You said ask."

"That was before I heard the question."

"The set up."

"Right. The set up."

"What's wrong? Is it the job? Is it me?"

I can see his mind churning away, the muscles in his temples working overtime, pumping blood wherever it's needed to think and mull over and come up with something clever. "I don't know what we're talking about," he says. "I'm sorry, I'm distracted. I've got a lot on my mind."

A car behind us honks. I glance back and see a string of polished sedans, all of them I imagine filled with antsy doctors and option traders and lewdly rich software developers. Maybe a rock star or two. The restaurant is in Rumson, the home to Springsteen, Bon Jovi, and Ojeda, a guy with a first name I never remember, a big-time pitcher with the Mets back in the 1980s, I think. Lots of other moneyed folk not used to waiting in line.

Paul frowns at me and holds my gaze. He says, "When you came by, I was probably at the warehouse." Then he wipes imaginary dust from the steering wheel and says, "What day was it?"

"Does it matter?"

"I was at the warehouse." He leans forward and to the side, stretching across my body, and rubs at the dash, way over in the corner on my side of the car, with his oatmeal-colored towel.

I look to my right through the large glass doors into the restaurant lobby and it is standing room only. "It looks busy."

He doesn't respond and doesn't look past me into the restaurant. All his attention is focused on wedging a corner of the towel into the seam around one of the knobs on the dash just below the air-conditioning vent, where I honestly doubt there's one speck of dirt. I ask, "Can you stop that for a moment?"

He leans back in his seat as if it takes great effort, and turns away from me looking out the driver's side window. "Do you think he's coming back?" he asks, meaning the valet kid.

"Let's leave it. Put the keys on the seat. I think he'll figure it out."

"I'm not sure," he says, which means, "No way in hell am I leaving the keys to the S-Class to some snot-nosed kid in high school even if I have to sit here all night."

I breathe in deeply, let it out and absently reach over and touch a shiny chrome section of the gearshift. "You never answered my question."

He wants to wipe down the gearshift knob where I touched it. He doesn't, but he wants to. "I thought I did."

"Something's wrong. Okay, not wrong, but different."

He can't sit still and rotates his entire body away from me, pressing the side of his head to the driver side window. "He's not coming back."

"What are you hiding?"

Paul fiddles with the cloth in his hands.

"You can tell me," I say.

"I can, can I?"

"You'll feel better if you do. I promise."

"If I tell you, I'll feel better."

"I promise." I say, and in that moment I see a possible opening.

"There he is," Paul shouts with an excess of enthusiasm. He reaches for the door release and pushes the door open, changes his mind, leans into the car and wipes down the wood trim around the radio, GPS and the 500 tiny knobbies surrounding the screen. He wipes the gearshift knob, then jams the towel in his pocket and gets out of the car.

The following week Paul disappears. He's gone for days, five if it matters. When he returns I look him in the eye, and to show I'm as independent as the next woman, I *don't* pressure him for details. I do ask where he skipped off to, hoping for some plausible explanation, but I ask it as indifferently as asking a six-year-old if he's been drinking out of the milk carton again when you know damn well he has, though he says, "Nope. Not me." Those are the kind of words I expect to hear from Paul, but he's jittery and can't keep his stories this short. He elaborates and builds layers of cause and effect and a massive cast of characters each connected to others in madcap ways, and suddenly I feel I'm playing a bit part in a *Lifetime* movie. My boyfriend is up to no good and has a screwy way of keeping it a secret.

As for the rise-and-shine, I've-got-to-get-up-early-and-get-to-work attitude he oozed when we first met, none of it remains. In fact, it appears he doesn't work at all. I casually mention the food business and he grows sullen, evasive. I bring up the office, appointments, paperwork - isn't there some place he's supposed to be during the day - and he glares at me. So I stop asking. He has recently sold a home, he tells me, so money isn't a problem, which would have been a spot-on reply had I asked about cash flow and the source of his bottomless pit.

A couple of weeks later, disappearance number two. This time four days.

When it comes up later he talks and talks as if I've hit the on switch. I have no idea how to turn him off. He brings me a bowl of ice cream and accuses me of sleeping around. The following day, I catch him rummaging through my purse looking for proof that there's someone else.

About this time, I'm on a business trip selling insurance to a gaggle of smiling Texans, and I get a text message on my phone.

He's mine, so leave him alone.

I figure it's a wrong number. Then I get another.

He loves me not you. Butt out.

And another.

I know he's told you about me. I'm his ex. The one he really loves.

I don't bother to text back. What would I say?

But they keep coming.

We're in love. You don't get it do you?

And—

You're ruining everything.

When I return, I confront him. Paul confirms the messages are from his ex-girlfriend, but swears on his sacred cap and gown photo that he's done with her. No idea how she got my phone number. Absolutely no clue why the texts started while I was out of town. Paul puts an arm around me. "It's over. Trust me."

Paul's mom visits shortly after my return from Texas. I confided in her about the messages. She doesn't miss a beat. "The poor woman is not right. I wouldn't worry about it, if I were you." But I can't escape it.

Every five or six days I get another text.

Stay away.

Sometimes in the middle of the night.

I'm warning you.

I ring Tonya, my best friend, and tell her about Paul, about the erratic behavior and accusations, the jitters and the speed-talking. I tell her about the text messages.

"How long has he acted this way?" she asks, probably rolling her eyes.

"I didn't mark it on the calendar."

"Venture a guess."

"I think it started maybe a few weeks ago, about two months after we started dating."

"Let me get this straight. For two months he was normal. Nothing weird. Then one day he gets the heebie-jeebies and they never go away?"

"And way talkative."

Tonya blows into the phone in a way she knows I hate. "Drugs," she says and I expect to hear a "Duh?" but don't.

"I don't see it," I say.

"Cocaine," she says matter of fact. "Deny it if it makes you feel better. But he's knee deep in it, judging from what you just told me, and nothing you believe or don't believe will make a bit of difference."

"What about the text messages?"

"The next time you get one, reply. Tell her she can have him back."

It's true, of course. Paul is a druggy or an addict or one of the levels in between and everyone can see it but me. I ask around and find out that his business dealings are "shady" at best. And, in addition to the ex, who he's bonking with some regularity, I have anecdotal evidence he's sleeping around with one, probably two, others.

I'm ashamed. Embarrassed. Humiliated. I can't think of a word worse than humiliated, but if there is one, insert it here.

I'm a fool.

I call Tonya every day and bawl until I run out of tears or my throat goes scratchy or my voice fades altogether, whichever comes first, and I deny all of it. It's a phase, I tell her, and all relationships go through this. Other days I call and cry and set the denial aside for a time. I shake my head at the phone, unbelieving just how stupid one person, me, can be. After a dozen such calls, I'm spent. Depleted. Used up. I decide it's time for a new environment. I need a fresh start. This is no time to ponder. It's time to act (before I change my mind). My company has satellite offices across the country and I look up the one farthest from here. I muster a spoonful of courage, rehearse what I'm about to say, decide an impromptu strategy is likely more effective, and approach my boss.

I market insurance products, "Something I can do anywhere," I tell him. "I'm single and just turned thirty-nine, and I need a change. West," I say as if this one word explains everything. This is possibly the most unconvincing argument I can make and it goes nowhere. He's baffled and confused about just where this is coming from. The conversation takes a while. I do a lousy job of explaining myself, my logic is faulty, and for brief periods I don't make the slightest sense. Not a good combination if you want your company to pony up airfare and moving expenses or at a minimum to keep paying you on time. After a little wrangling, my boss stops talking and I get emotional and cry. Then I get a thought.

I ask what he thinks of the idea of having a presence, possibly an office, in Northern California.

"How northern?" he asks.

"San Francisco. The entire Bay Area. It's an enormous market," I say.

"I hear the cost of living is outrageous."

"Is that a no?" I ask.

He doesn't care about the cost and we both know it. He's thinking about new clients and company growth and cash flow. He is far from shocked by my suggestion. He leans back in his leather chair and I detect an earnest longing in the way he rubs the lobe of his ear, playing out viable alternatives in his head. Here he has a willing guinea pig to go scout new territory.

"I hear Napa is beautiful this time of year," he says. "While you're out there you could take a little trip north and check out the wine country. What is it, an hour and a half?"

"Forty-eight miles," I say. "I'm way ahead of you."

I get my transfer.

A fresh start. New friends. Concentrate on work, I tell myself, and forget about Paul. It's a good plan.

I speak with my landlord and sever my lease. Three days from now, on Monday, I'll fly out to California and return on Friday. While I'm there, I'll look around, check out the office, find a place to live, come home, pack and begin my new life. I call Tonya from the office and tell her the good news. She's pouty about my moving so far away, but agrees it's probably for the best. To compensate for skedaddling off to sunny California, I agree to visit her in Maryland over the weekend. I'll hop in my car and cruise down the New Jersey turnpike and arrive Friday noonish. On Sunday afternoon, I'll do the trip in reverse. The following day, I'll catch a plane to California, look for a place and start my new life. It's all set.

For a solid twenty minutes I'm this close to feeling splendid about life. Then I pull into the parking garage of my condo. It's late and much of the place is shadowy, most of it an ugly brown-gray fading to black, not the pretty blue-gray of ocean sunsets. That's when I see my ex, the big sneak, doing a lousy job of concealing himself behind a concrete column in a semi-lit section of the garage not far from the elevators. I get out of my car and chirp once for lock. When I get close to the elevator Paul pops out from his hiding place like a cartoon character. I'm not so much scared as annoyed.

"You forgot your cape," I say.

"You can't hide from me," he says. His hands shake and he doesn't know whether to shove them in his pockets or hide them behind his back. Or possibly give them something to grab hold of, like my neck where they will squeeze until the shaking goes away.

"I live here," I say. "You were very clever to track me down."

"You've got a mouth on you."

"What do you want?" I ask in a voice almost bored and thus intended to drive Paul batty.

"This isn't going to happen," he says.

"You don't look too good," I say.

"Whatever you think you're up to," he says, running his words together, "it's not gonna work."

"Are you drunk?" I ask, but this isn't drink. It's drugs of one flavor or another. Even I can see it now.

"What I do is none of your concern," he says.

"Is there any chance I can hurry this along?"

Paul takes a step forward and stumbles. He rights himself and grins at me the way he used to back when things were good and we didn't meet late at night in darkened parking garages. "We were something together."

"You and I are over," I say. "I don't care about you anymore," and the moment I hear myself say this, the words sound small, almost childlike. And just that fast an iota of confidence slips away. It's tiny, trivial even, but I can feel it go. It all happens so quickly I'm caught off guard and I know with aching certainty that more will follow. "I'm talking to you out of courtesy," I say "so don't confuse this with anything more."

"This?"

"If I have to explain 'this' then we don't have much left to say."

Hold on, I tell myself and I involuntarily mouth the words. Hold on. Hold on. I stare at Paul's shaky hands, at the large veins in his neck, but first I look around and see a couple of other people still in the parking garage, a man leaning inside his trunk tugging on a box and a woman walking away from us with a briefcase in her hand.

"No one leaves *me*," he says, words running together. He's tired. Or the drugs are losing steam or something else is happening. I want no part of it. "That doesn't happen to *me*," he says.

"I need to get going."

"All show, that's what you are." Paul's voice is husky and mean. The longer he talks the louder he gets. "You had a good thing with me. You may not want to admit it," he barks at me, "but without me you're nothing."

A man in a jogging suit and a cardboard box in his hands walks by and pauses, his eyes on me. Without thinking, I give him a subtle headshake. I don't need any help with this one, the shake says. The next moment, I wish I could take it back. The man watches Paul for a moment and hitches up the box in his hands and picks up the pace and keeps moving. Paul stares at the man's back and contorts his face.

Angry wrinkles form on his forehead. To me he says, "You'll never amount to nothing."

"Is that so?"

"You can't just walk away." He shakes his head in a wide exaggerated motion, the antagonistic wrinkles in his forehead growing deeper. "You think you can and you're wrong. You don't have it in you. Do, and you'll grow old and lonely, but it doesn't matter because I know you. I know all about women like you and you can't do it."

Something inside me falls into place. Click. At first I think of a penny landing in dirt. No, that's not right. It's not a click and not dirt but closer to a worn deadbolt sliding into place, the kind that often make barely a sound. Some gear or cog or a hardened piece of my own thought process finally finds a home. Some sliver of self-awareness surfaces and rotates itself over and allows me to see the world from a new perspective, maybe as it really is, or at least from an angle so new and foreign and oddly oblique that what I see right now, in this very instant, is nothing like what I saw a moment ago. Me. Paul. The dimly lit garage and its place in the world. It's all changed. All this takes less than a second. A half second. A half, half second.

"Keep your eyes on this," I say and turn and take a step. "This is me walking away." I get ten feet from Paul and don't turn or slow. "I don't want to see you again. Ever."

I enter the elevator and push the button. I feel the floor push on my feet. I wait for the motion to stop. I count to three and the doors open on cue. I walk down the carpeted hallway and unlock the door to my condominium. I take a step inside, close the door, lock it and stand there just inside with the lights off and count until I realize I've stopped counting. I'm finished with tears, I tell myself. And bad men. I am positively finished with bad men. I make a pact with myself, standing there in my entryway without light. This is my pact: No one will ever again speak to me that way. No one will scare me silly. No one will run me down. No one will treat me as a possession, even an elegant possession. Here's the big one, the reason people make pacts with themselves: No one will stand between my desire and me. I deserve better. I'm worthy of better. For the first time in a long time, I believe in myself. I'm attractive and smart, have a job and a handful of genuine friends. I'm me. Here's the thing: I'm okay with that.

No sooner do I arrive in Maryland, Tonya needs a favor. She's woozy with the flu or some other irksome illness and needs me to do this one little thing. Can I drop off her daughter, Gina, at one of her friends? Tonya is a good mom and she hasn't met Ashley, Gina's new friend, nor Ashley's divorced father, so she wants me to go rap on the door and have a look-see.

"Sure," I say, "why not?"

Ashley's father, Rick, answers the door. He looks nice and harmless enough. He invites me inside. I step into a stunning two-month old condo on Assawoman Bay just outside of Ocean City, Maryland. Rick is newly divorced and he bought the place, he tells me, because it's close to his kids' school. He has partial custody of his children (Matthew a sullen fifteen, Ashley a chirpy thirteen, and Connor eleven) every other weekend and having a local condo seemed like the perfect place to gather for a couple of weekends a month. The back of the home is filled with large windows that look out on the bay. Every room is filled with hardwood floors, crown molding, and walls of glass. A chandelier over the dining room table catches my eye. It reminds me of a gigantic dragonfly with its shiny eyes lighting up the room. We talk about the light and the view and, for no reason I can think of, I tell him I'd just ended a relationship.

"Oh," he says.

"And I'm moving to California."

We talk and talk. Whenever I sense an awkward silence looming near, I talk some more. An hour passes without my noticing and it's time to hustle back to Tonya and give her my report. The father: safe, not a wacko, easy to talk to, attractive, not really my type. This is the Friday before the Super Bowl. On Saturday Gina calls her mom from Ashley's and asks if she and I would like to have lunch with the three of them— Gina, Ashley, and Rick.

Tonya and I zip over to a local Italian joint. Throughout lunch the girls giggle, purring to each other like contented kittens. It strikes me that these two are nosing Rick and me closer. Meanwhile before the girls left, unknown to me, one or both of them had written my name and cell phone number on a handful of sticky notes using the big loopy lettering of happy teens. The notes have an abundance of hearts and stars around the edges. When Rick returns, he notices the notes plastered all over the condo, on the walls and doors and kitchen appliances. In a sense, the girls intuit something I don't. They understand that Rick and I need a nudge. He's a very nice guy, but different from the men I date. He's reserved, conservative, and a doctor, the sort who tinkers with hearts in what I imagine is the objective, detached way my dentist gleefully drills holes in my teeth. I think about it for a minute then remember. Monday I'm out of here.

The following day I hear Tonya on the phone and one-sided as it is, I get that Rick is planning to drop Gina at Tonya's house later that evening. I get the notion it might be better if I'm not here when he arrives. It's not that I don't want to see him. It is, well, sort of the opposite. After everything I had just gone through I want to play hard to get, and I want to see if Rick has any interest in "getting" me, and if so, how hard is he going to try? Will he make an excuse to drop by again? Will he call? Or is he one of those men who lets fate decide his future, the kind who meets a curvy blonde they are attracted to and do little or nothing about it. He's a doctor and I've no way of knowing how doctors go about pulling women into their world, if they even do such things.

When Rick arrives, I decide to be gone. And that's that.

In Napa, I cruise Silverado Trail in my rental. A stand of big-leaf maple and bay laurel throws long shadows across the road. I'm on my way to one of my favorite places on Earth, Auberge du Soleil, an unpretentious but luxurious country inn and spa overlooking the Napa Valley. I'm all by my lonesome and looking forward to stretching out on one of those padded tables and having my body kneaded and plied like a lump of sculptor's clay about to be molded into something breathtaking. I'd been here before, years earlier, a time in my life when I'd visited California to survive the madness of my job and New Jersey in general.

Auberge du Soleil is clad in aged, graying wood siding and split wood shingles half covered by climbing ivy and overhanging trees. From the front, the place looks of the earth rather than manmade. I'm about to park when my phone rings.

"Do you know who this is?" a voice asks.

I pull into a parking spot and kill the engine. "I do," I say. It's Rick. I can tell by the voice, smooth and confident with a hint of an east coast accent.

He makes chitchat for a moment or two, and then says, "I've got an event coming up. It's kind of a big deal. I was wondering if you'd care to accompany me."

"What is it, this big event of yours?"

"The Heart Ball." As a heart doc, Rick is more or less required to make an appearance. He tries to make the evening sound, if not exactly a blast, at least not a bore. The ball is an annual event, formal, and takes place this coming weekend.

"Let me think about it," I say.

We chat. I tell him I'm dying to get inside and grab a glass of wine and get in line for a massage.

"Yeah, okay," he says. "Think about it." And we hang up.

My strategy worked. Play hard to get and some men won't bother. Others, like Rick, seem to take it in stride. Standing there in the parking lot of this charming hilltop getaway, I'm not sure how I feel about Rick, the Heart Ball, or any of it. I'm only weeks away from a relationship. Does it make any sense to leap into another?

I stroll through the rustic front doors of Auberge du Soleil and within twenty minutes am face down on a masseuse's table being pushed and prodded by an expert. After, I have dinner at the Auberge restaurant. The place is rich with muted earth colors, exposed beams, and woodsy furniture. I order lobster bisque and stare glassy-eyed at the massive wine menu. My waitress, a delicate girl who marches when she walks, looks me over and suggests the Elan 2001 Cabernet Sauvignon. She describes it as multi-layered. Sort of chocolaty and spicy with a hint of tobacco, sage, and mint. A glass of the Elan costs twice my entree, but I order it anyway and it's delicious. I sip my wine and look out over the vineyards. When I'm good and ready, I reach into my purse for my phone, punch in a number, and when Rick answers, I say, "I'd be honored to attend the Heart Ball."

Chapter Three

Stumbling Upon a Prince

··

T he Heart Ball is February 12, 2005, and as I get ready I recall the last thing Rick said to me on the phone. It came off as an afterthought, but I think he planned it that way. "Wear something conservative," he had said. What would he think I'd wear, a studded mini?

After my long drive from New Jersey back to Maryland, Rick picks me up at Tonya's house, and by the time he arrives I'm primped, pampered, and waiting. I bought a new dress before leaving California. I'd settled on a stretch high neck sleeveless dress with matching crop jacket and high black pumps. The outfit is conservative but sexy. I peek out the window and see Rick strolling up the walk in a trim fitting black suit. He looks good, tall and handsome. It's six weeks after Christmas and Tonya still has a large Santa in the yard. It's nice as lawn decorations go, all steel and beautifully hammered metal with lights around the edges of Santa's coat and hat. Rick stops and stares at the Santa for a moment. He glances up the block and across the street and then back to the Santa. Not another Christmas decoration in sight. I know what he's thinking. He knocks and Tonya answers the door and the first thing he says is, "Don't you think it's time to retire the Santa?" A man who speaks his mind, even when it's inappropriate. Already I like him more than I first thought.

Tonya frowns. She considers the remark rude.

Later, in the car, I say, "That wasn't nice."

"It's February," he says.

"It still wasn't nice."

My high heels give me a little nervous twitch. I kick at a paper wrapper on the floorboard of Rick's SUV. "Tell me more about the ball," I say. "What am I getting myself into?"

"You'll have fun," he says not really answering my question. "I promise."

"It's a secret, is that it?"

Rick just shakes his head and grabs my hand, without words accompanying.

His car is a dump. An old, dirty SUV. One of those models that looks like every other SUV. I'm used to men with nice cars. Yet even if his is old, shouldn't it be cleaned and shined like someone just buffed the bejesus out of it? Here's my big date with a doctor who shows up in a heap. Part of me thinks, "This can't be his only car". He *has* to have another car somewhere, in the shop, loaned out to a desperate friend. Something. The heap *is* his only car, I find out later. Up to then, he had owned a total of three cars in his life. I don't consider myself a car nut. I don't fall in love with them, but I've certainly owned more than three cars in my life. And, I know where the closest car wash is. He's consistent, I'll give him that much. The suit, once I get a closer look, reminds me of the car: it is a single-breasted jacket with wide shoulders and all of it is dizzyingly wrinkled. Not the big wrinkles of trendy Italian linen, but the more mundane everyday crinkles of a man too absorbed in the big picture—fixing weakened hearts and blocked arteries and saving lives—to give a hoot about attending a fancy function in crumpled clothes.

He looks cute, nonetheless. And I like him. I can wash the SUV, or better, convince him to buy something with a bit more swank. I can press the suit. What is a whole lot more difficult is finding a man who cares more about the stuff on the inside—and here I'm referring to purpose, values and doing good—than clean cars and wrinkle-free suits.

The ball is held in a large, bayside restaurant in Dewey Beach, Delaware. When we arrive, there are more than two hundred happy doctors, businessmen, and spouses milling around shaking hands, patting backs, and moving their bodies on the dance floor. I don't know these people or this world, but I'm in sales and I make a living by talking to people. Talking, I can do anywhere, anytime. If Rick leaves me unattended, I introduce myself to the nearest person and we're off. How long had Rick and I dated? Where had we met? What was Rick really like away from his office? I answer all takers with the unvarnished truth. "We've dated for, well, let's see," I glance at my watch, "for about two hours if you count the time in the car on our way here. We met at his condo in West Ocean City, Maryland. And as for what he's like outside the office, I've never seen him *in* the office, so I've nothing to compare to."

My party banter is well honed and I hum along making new friends. I sip my glass of California Chardonnay. In fact, I have only a single glass the entire ball. Rick, on the other hand, is in a mood. He is giddy with life, me, and his friends at the ball. And to accompany that giddiness, he tosses back one scotch and then another. The big event of the night is the silent charity auction. Rick and I inspect the auction items. He spots several things he likes and one in particular he has to have, a large ceramic iguana with clear brown eyes, green lizardy skin, and a mouth clamped shut in a perpetual grin.

He asks me to dance. We do and we meet more people. Before I know it, I'm having a time. The evening is not what I'm used to. I'm accustomed to more noise and clashing bodies and the sense that something unexpected might rise up and surprise you. The Heart Ball is not a place for the unexpected. Its charm is in knowing what's about to happen, which is nosey spouses looking for gossip, lots of staid professional voices—mostly men, though not all—and the occasional revelation. Nevertheless, I feel comfortable with these people and with

Rick. We dance some more and talk some more and when the auction is over—and sadly Rick has *not* won his nubby ceramic iguana—we wander outside and down the beach to a little bar on the water. It's a quaint little place, small and artsy. There are six of us there on bar stools. The others, one woman and three men, glance at Rick and me with cheery disinterest. Rick, I can tell, isn't a seasoned drinker and all the single malts are catching up to him. He orders another and I have my second Chardonnay.

We speak in low voices, me prying him for information, changing topics whenever the conversation lags, and Rick happily telling stories complete with details and tangents that I now know is his trademark storytelling style. Rick is a born narrator, much better than me. He remembers small, particular details and he uses exacting words like "towering shagbark hickories" and "thousand yard stare" and "old rickety planes, Greyhounds of the skies" to make his point. I tend to summarize. I condense. I stick to the facts I can remember and often remember only a Reader's Digest version of events. Rick, on the other hand, either has a spectacular memory (not uncommon for a doctor), or he embellishes his stories for the sheer pleasure of it. Either way, I sip my wine and survey neat rows of Scotch and Bourbon and other distinctively shaped bottles behind the bar. Whenever the conversation takes a u-turn and meanders my way I ask another question. Rick talks and talks and drinks his whiskey. He is vulnerable and willing to share and I take advantage of the opportunity.

He'd stuck out a bad marriage for fourteen years. The two called it quits a couple of years earlier and the divorce took a surprising emotional toll on him. That, and it was costly. When it was all over, his ex despised him and proved it by poisoning his children in subtle yet powerful ways. The ex had a way of planting the seeds of anger and rage in her kids, especially Matthew, who at thirteen when the divorce was final needed only a direction to point his adolescent angst. "That's the reason for all your frustration and clumsiness and longing," the ex seemed to say. "That's the man responsible for all your moodiness and fading ego identity. Oh, and you can blame him for those pimples, as well."

Rick did all he could to preserve his relationship with his children. Through it all, and without really noticing, he had stopped eating, lost a ton of weight, and ended up depressed and consulting a psychiatrist to help put most of the pieces back together. The psychiatrist wasn't so much a counselor as a follower of the new school of psychiatry, who believed the right meds in the right dose at the right intervals can cure most that ails you. It was a lot to accomplish. Nevertheless, Rick's psychiatrist had a determined attitude and eventually found an anti-depressant that initially seemed effective but later weighed anchor on Rick's notoriously good judgment. For those few months after the divorce, the way Rick tells it, logic had flown the coop. Reason no longer had a dominant place in his personal life. During this period Rick dated a woman who finagled him into forking over half a mil to build condos on the water that, not surprisingly, never got built. He describes this disaster and I listen with rapt attention, occasionally nodding or tilting my head at a consoling slant or sometimes prompting him to go on. And he does.

There is something invigorating about hearing a life described in such an accelerated way. As if the simplicity of the telling is more truthful than the long version with all its excuses and convoluted justifications. Listening to Rick talk openly, though sometimes in a whisper so as not to disturb our bar mates, makes me think about my own life, the stories I might tell in this vividly unvarnished way. My story can wait. Tonight is about Rick. He lives in a structured world where you keep embarrassing anecdotes on the inside, where you may occasionally spill your guts, but never to anyone close, assuming you had anyone close to spill to, which Rick doesn't. He doesn't have many close friends, certainly not a confidant willing or interested enough to lift some of the burden, even for a few fleeting minutes. I am a stranger. I am safe. I don't know a soul in his life. So I get to hear the parts of his life he's never shared with anyone other than his shrink, though I can't be sure. Rick fought his demons, got battered in the process, and survived. Here is a man who strikes me as something special. Here is a wonderful man.

I know something about good men. My first marriage was to a good man, though during that marriage I still felt something was missing. It lasted four good years and ended, as ending marriages do, on a less than positive note. After, I dated a couple of men whom I choose to describe as dubious, men with syrupy voices and suspiciously incomplete life stories. Men who have a history of avoiding encumbrances and complicated relationships. You don't see them as untrustworthy right away, or at least I didn't, but the clues begin to mount. Some men are evil, there's no denying it, and that evil comes in all shapes and disguises. One pattern of evil, if there is a pattern, is that of men with glitz and glam on the outside who go to great lengths to avoid letting you see even a smidgen of what's on the inside.

Rick is the opposite.

He isn't glitz. He doesn't obstruct.

On the contrary, he is consummate player-by-the-rules. In Rick I see honesty like nothing I'd experienced in my previous six years since my divorce. He is genuine and offers me a peek at the inside. You could say he may have forced me to look, but however you cut it, what I see is what I've come to regard as my highest praise where men are concerned—Rick is a good man.

He has one free weekend a month; a weekend without children, without waiting by the phone for a call from the hospital or a desperate patient, and this is that weekend.

After the ball, the cozy little bar, and the drive home, we pull up to the condo, shuffle inside, kiss in the doorway, kiss again in the kitchen and throughout the night.

The following day, I stroll back to Tonya's around eleven o'clock. This is Sunday and Tonya is mildly aggravated with me for not calling to say I hadn't been murdered, abandoned, or chopped into pieces and fed to a school of tuna cruising the mouth of Assawoman Bay. Tonya is a worrier. I pacify her with small talk and tell her I'll be out of her hair soon because Rick is picking me up in a couple of hours. To say Rick and I hit it off right away doesn't come close. It's more intense than that. The only minor snag is that committed-to job in California.

At lunch Rick and I mull over the awkward timing of my job transfer and our newfound relationship.

"Why don't you stick around for a while," Rick says.

"What, like go to my boss and tell him I've changed my mind?"

"You have, haven't you?"

"That's not the point. I'll look unprofessional. I'll look like a flake."

"Don't say that."

"Besides, I need to get out of New Jersey." I tell Rick about the relationship with P. (I can't force myself to say his name for fear of some cosmic repercussions.) I explain that I'm angry with myself for not immediately recognizing his despicable character, and am trying, somewhat frantically, to distance myself from him. I say that as much as I hate admitting such things, I feel dazed. Not the kind of mild confusion that an extra strength Tylenol might just cure, but another kind, the cloudy, disorienting loss of purpose. And I don't seem to have the energy to focus on anything. This is my version of dazed, when I'm not drawn to anything or anyone (or I wasn't until a few hours ago) and thus find myself moving through the days feeling bruised and muddle-headed.

"I need distance," I say to Rick, who is staring at me, casually focused on my words, not even bothering to pick at his roast beef with Muenster. "Three thousand miles sounds just about right."

He lifts his sandwich but doesn't take a bite. "Move into my condo?"

"You don't even know me," I say.

Off my look, he says, "Not my house." He smiles, bites into the sandwich, chews for longer than necessary, and says, "I'm not asking you to move in with me. I mean the condo in West Ocean City where I meet the kids every couple of weeks. It's empty but for a few days a month. Take some time. You don't need 3,000 miles to think."

"What about the kids?"

"They're never there."

"It sounds like a bad idea."

"The price is right."

"A really, really bad idea."

"Look for a job around Ocean City, or closer to my home in Delaware. What do you have to lose?"

Rick is right of course.

His logic skills are kicking in big time, and we both know it. I didn't have a thing to lose. Maybe Maryland is far enough away from Jersey. My intuition has been telling me Rick is a good man. And not a week has gone by that I didn't hear from a headhunter tempting me with the offer of a better job. The economy is good. What the hell. Why not?

On Monday, I hightail it out of Maryland at five-thirty in the morning and make it into work in New Jersey by nine. First thing, I call my boss. He is out of town and won't be back for several days. I need to take action or risk doing nothing at all, so I dial the human resources director and tell her I've changed my mind about the job in California. In fact, I'd changed my mind about a lot of things and I resign my position. The HR director is pissed off, but she is also a professional and she asks what is going on. I don't need to, but I tell her about my hateful ex-boyfriend, that I'm stressed to the breaking point, and that I need time and space between me and my ex. I explain my embarrassment, my need for a new start, and politely offer my two weeks. After that I'm gone.

I've worked since I was fourteen and don't plan to stop any time soon. I like the independence working affords me. I like to have my own, and I like to make my own. Thankfully, I was able to collect unemployment (how that happened I don't know) but lucky me, so I don't panic and instead enjoy a few weeks of leisure time. With all this freedom on my hands, I decide to give Rick and me a try. I don't want to be the dependent new girlfriend, so I begin looking for an inexpensive condo nearby. Tonya has a friend in real estate and with help, I find a condo right on Assawoman Bay in the same development as Rick's condo, Tonya's home, and my ex in-laws' home (if you can believe that), in the quaint town of West Ocean City, Maryland.

The community includes a pristine nine-mile stretch of bay front, 7,000 homes, a couple of hundred condo units, four outdoor pools, golf course, tennis complex, two marinas, yacht club, the whole shebang. My chosen is in a flamingo-pink building. The inside is basically a dump, but within walking distance of the yacht club, which is a plus. Rick is enthusiastic about the move and commits to helping me fix up the place. He sends over the interior designer who worked his magic on his home in Delaware and I begin scribbling notes as we walk the condo, pointing and talking in clipped, rapid-fire fashion.

While waiting to close on the condo, I move all my things into storage. Rick, the perpetual look-three-steps-ahead guy that he is, suggests that I move most of my clothes into his Delaware home until my place is ready.

Between resigning my position at work and closing on the condo, I get my first look at his primary home in Delaware, a massive brick colonial right on the river. He had paid dearly to keep the house when he and his ex divorced. It is close to the hospital and besides, the ex now lives in the beach house, a gorgeous 6,000-square-foot oceanfront home Rick had designed and built himself. The Delaware home is all hardwood floors, granite countertops, and wood moldings. I spot a Chatsworth accent chair and leather ottoman and an American Revival dining room table. I'm impressed. Rick points me upstairs where I can move my clothes. The closets and storage space are thankfully enough to hold my sizeable collection.

While work crews are going at my condo redecoration knee deep, tearing out the old and putting in the new, I spend my evenings with Rick. One night leads to two, which lead to three. I decide to show my appreciation to a man who has almost everything. I spend days thinking about an appropriate gift, something he won't toss in a drawer when I'm not looking. It comes to me. The handmade iguana he failed to win at the Heart Ball. Not something I'd normally go for, but it isn't for me, it's for him, and he liked it enough to plunk down a bid. I track the artist down and drive to his shop in Rehoboth Beach. Thankfully he has another.

Rick opens the package and eases out the ceramic lizard. He smiles at me and I know I did well.

We never acknowledge it, but I have moved in. By the time the condo is livable, I've lost all interest in my cute but tiny 800-square-foot shoebox. I've also changed my tune about maintaining my independence, at least as far as living arrangements are concerned. In the end, I don't spend a single night in my new condo.

In April, I accept a new job with a company that specializes in professional liability insurance, and although I now live in Delaware, my duty is to build up the New Jersey market. The best part is I get to work from home much of the week, making calls and setting up appointments. Then I hit the road, drive north on I-95 and meet prospective clients face-to-face in New Jersey. I work for two guys—the boss, a graying executive in a graying suit, and his number one, a little man who refuses to take off his police-officer style sunglasses regardless of the weather. It's far from perfect, but I'm working.

My life is like watching a movie in fast-forward. I meet Rick, turn down the job in California, buy a condo, accept a new job, restore the condo, and move in with Rick. We've known each other all of three months when I lay it out. "I want to be a mother. I'm thirty-nine," I say, as if that explains everything.

"I have three already," Rick says.

I stay silent, ruing the years I wasted when I could have been making babies. "I think we have a future together. Tell me if you think otherwise."

"Of course we do, and you want children?"

"If you don't want any more, just say so."

"I'm fifty."

"So," I say, "you're a young fifty…."

"I didn't do such a great job my first time around."

"With the kids you mean?"

"Three kids and a bad divorce. It takes its toll."

We talk for some time and eventually the conversation grinds to halt of its own weight.

When Ashley and Gina had merrily plastered my name and phone number around the condo, I'll bet they hadn't planned on this. The get-together. The serious talk about children. Fortunately Rick's children never come to the Delaware house because their school and all their friends are closer to the condo in West Ocean City. When he has the kids for the weekend, Rick and I take separate cars and trek southeast for the hour it takes to drive from Delaware to West Ocean City. For a while, at least, the kids don't know I'm "shacking up" with their father. It's our little secret. Later, it's harder to hide. As we get more serious, the kids start to react. On the outside, they are all smiles. On the inside, they seethe, act out, argue, and grow sullen and bitter. Immediately after the Heart Ball, Ashley was a joy to be around. Now she's pulled back to about a thousand feet and views me with a bird-watcher's detachment. Matthew knows what to think and it isn't good. Connor is eleven and still in that go-with-the-flow attitude that never lasts long enough. I get it. Rick's ex has worked her potions on them. She's poisoned them to mistrust their father and to hate me by association. The ex openly bad-mouths the father to his children in an effort to, I don't know what, make herself look like the good mother or play the victim.

I'm the new woman in their father's life. I expect some flack. Just not a never-ending vituperative downpour. Once, Rick and I and the kids drove up to see his mother in Pennsylvania, and along the way the kids were giggling in the back seat, making nonsensical murmurs and comments. I saw Rick gritting his teeth and not saying a word, staring fixedly at the highway. It was then I realized the kids were giving him a hard time in a way I wasn't meant to understand. Given that negative atmosphere, the unsympathetic grumblings all around us, and the odd nerviness in my lower belly, you'd think Rick and I would have put on the brakes, but we didn't. The craziness only made us stronger.

When it's time to renew my driver's license, Rick says, "Don't get your driver's license in Maryland. He's referring to the address of my condo and the logical address to put on my license.

"What are you suggesting?"

"Get it here in Delaware. Use my address. Our address."

"Why?"

"Insurance is less expensive," he says, and at the time it may have been.

Relationships, mine anyway, are like slogging through quicksand. With each step 10,000 tiny grains of sand engulf you. Changing the address on my license is one more speck of sand sucking me deeper into this relationship. And I can't wait.

Chapter Four

My Poet
....

In four months of living together, this is what I learn. Rick isn't polished. He isn't practiced at relationships. He isn't easily swayed and he isn't like any other man I've ever dated. On the other hand, he is good looking. Check. Tall. Check. Has all his hair. Check. He is a doctor who works long hours at a job he loves and never complains. He is intelligent and poised and thoughtful and only barely aware of the remarkable life he lives. A man who drives an eight-year-old Mercury Mountaineer, he tells me, because it's paid for and still runs. And while he isn't into cars, he is into property, a certain kind of property that involves being close to water. He adores oceanfront homes and riverfront homes and lake homes. All of it his idea of money well spent. Property is an appreciable asset, he tells me in that practiced voice I've grown to enjoy, if not love, a voice that can talk congenital heart defects and atrial flutter and property values and not leave you wanting to slit your wrist. "Waterfront property," he says, "it's going nowhere but up."

We sit out on the back patio of his home in Delaware, the one where I now live, watching the lazy waters of the Nanticoke River ease on by. The evening air is cool and damp. This is one of my favorite spots, sitting here on the large wooden deck, several feet above the yard, peeking through the evenly spaced wooden rails of the deck at the Nanticoke. The yard is wide and flat, precisely leveled, higher than the river by half a dozen feet, buttressed by a wall of wood, stone, or some other river-protecting material I can't see from here. Off to one side of the yard are two giant white ash trees with their crazy branches going every which way. Behind us, the back of the house is as comforting as a medieval castle with its walls of aged red brick and oversized windows.

"Why water?" I ask.

"What?" Rick says.

"Why the infatuation with water?"

"I'm not sure," he says.

"Is it just money or is there more?"

Rick looks over at me to see what I'm driving at, studies me as if I were one of his patients, trying to understand what's really behind my words.

I raise my wine glass. "Are you getting up?" We sit in lounge chairs facing the freshly mowed lawn, my chair sort of skewed, pointing at the larger of the two ash trees, Rick's exactingly perpendicular to the edge of the deck, parallel to the rows of rusted nail heads, and more or less aligned with the world. Rick wears a pair of old jeans and a tee shirt, the kind of man who grows more handsome with age, who becomes stately over time and then one day you see it, sort of suddenly, and you appreciate it all the more. I can't tell if I'm the only one to witness this transformation of the slightly invisible, hardworking doctor into the stately man sitting next to me, but I do witness it. I glance at him when he stares at the water and what I see in these moments is precious, as if I've misplaced something wonderful and irreplaceable and now I've found it. I see the man next to me as clearly as I see the long blades of the manicured lawn, the clumps of saw grass at the river's edge, the gray-brown river itself, and the dense giant sumac and red maple trees lining the river on the other side.

"I think some of my best memories involve water," he says. "When I was a child I spent days at the Jersey Shore, walking through the sand and along the beach. I remember the dark rocks the size of small cars along the jetties. Each year, my family spent a week at the Shore."

"And you liked it?" I ask.

He is fair-skinned, assertive in a way that is subtle and forceful at the same time. "I had fun there. I was at peace. I didn't appreciate my life much back then, but I liked the Shore."

I turn and smile as if this is a joke, but it isn't.

"It was freedom to me. When we were at the beach, I didn't have to, I don't know— Nothing was expected of me. It was me and the beach and the ocean."

I glance at my empty glass of wine. "Are you getting up?"

"In a minute," he says and I can see he wants to talk.

"The water was a source of joy and happiness for me." He speaks in a wistful far-away voice. He brushes something off the front of his tee shirt, he tells me about taking the job here in Delaware when he finished up his cardiology fellowship. It was a big decision, to join a group practice or go it alone. After interviewing with a handful of groups, he was pretty sure he didn't want to be the third, fourth, or fifth man on the totem pole, the partners telling him, years down the road, whether he'd make partner or not. He decided to make his own way and started work at a small hospital in southern Delaware, right here in the town where we live, a hospital in desperate need of a cardiologist.

"The town was pretty close to the beach," he says. "I knew I wanted to build a beach place and spend my weekends there. The town had a river running though it and I figured someday, I'd get a place on the river."

"So you landed here because of the ocean and the river?"

On the river an old white tug is pushing a less than enthusiastic rusting barge up river to who knows where. The tug's motor is muffled, coming at us in waves of white noise. I can see a series of tires tied to the side in the charming way tug boat captain's string old tires about like year-round Christmas ornaments. The water turns white at the back of the tug and I detect the faint scent of whatever tugs use for fuel.

"Indirectly," Rick says. "The main thing was the job. The hospital gave me an income guarantee for the first year or two. It gave me some time to start a practice. And they needed a cardiologist." Rick gazes pensively out at the tug and barge combination. "I don't think I would have gone for it had it been in landlocked Ohio."

"Where do they go?" I ask, meaning the barges.

"Down river," he says rocking forward in his chair to get a closer look. "Sharpton, Riverton. Maybe all the way to Pocomoke Sound, the Chesapeake Bay. Up river, I think we're about it."

I think seriously of going to the kitchen and pouring another glass of wine, but don't want to lose the thread of our conversation, a thread that's getting thinner and thinner. "Go on," I say.

A year after he arrived, a developer started a new development on the Nanticoke River, and Rick was one of the first to tromp through the scrub, long before any roads were plowed, quickly putting his money down on two side-by-side lots. Three years later he built the home I now live in. He knew what he wanted out of life, a mere handful of things, and for those handfuls, he was as focused and aware as any anthropologist scouring the dusty remains of some lost culture. For most other things, however, like the clothes he wore, the cars he drove, and the hundreds of daily activities going on around him, he was oblivious. Exactly the kind of man I could marry.

I also learn that Rick is a romantic, the kind of old school romantic who not only feels romance but also expresses it. I remember a note he once wrote, a note I still have. I'd joined him at a medical conference in Philadelphia, where he was listening to men ramble about biomarkers and medical management and revascularization while I roamed the streets of Philly, window-shopping. We met just after a session on "Cardiomyopathies" and before a no-doubt rousing lecture on "New Antithrombotics." We were standing in a wide hallway on lush carpet waiting for a covey of doctors to politely shove their way into the conference room when Rick handed me a small piece of paper. He scooted inside. I stood there next to the double doors sinking into the cut pile, unfolded the note, and read.

> *As I sit here listening and the words garble and the images blur, before I slump into unconsciousness, I thought I'd pen you a note. I'm thinking of how much you mean to me, how much fun we had last night. You've become my soul mate—my best friend, partner, and lover. When we first met, I was taken by your beauty and sexiness (which, by the way, I appreciate more each day), but now I see more. I see what a truly giving and wonderful person you are. You work hard at our relationship. I accept that this means you love me, that our relationship means something to you. The same is true with me. It's almost impossible for me to imagine life without you.*

There's more, but I stopped, took a breath, and fanned my face with the flimsy paper. I was sort of swooning there, reading the words my beau had dreamed up to share with me. I glanced up just in time to see a cute bellboy coming at me fast, pulling a wheeled cart stuffed with a mountain of Louis Vuitton bags. At the last moment, I moved back a step. The bellboy rushes past and only then looked back at me and smiled. I went back to reading my note.

> *Things will never be the same since I've experienced our life together. I believe as we get to know each other, our relationship and love will grow. I know we make an unbelievable team.*

Then in smaller handwriting at the bottom of the page, scribbled there as an afterthought, or as if in secret code between the two of us, he wrote, *"Our romance has been fantastic. I'm fairly reserved, but I love you very much. I promise to look for more ways to let you know."*

A cool seven months into our new relationship, in August, we have the talk. It goes something like this. I say, "Look, neither of us is getting any younger."

"I'm listening," Rick says.

"We don't have a lot of time to waste."

"Couldn't agree more."

"I want kids, one, two, I don't know for sure, but I want them."

"Okay," he says.

"Okay what?"

"Okay, let's make a baby."

"Like that?" I say ready to fight and apparently no one willing to take me up on it.

"Well…."

There is only one tiny problem to this rosy picture of bliss. Rick's vasa deferentia have been snipped and tied. The two miniscule ducts, connecting the left and right epididymis to the ejaculatory ducts (this is Rick talking) have been clipped, and to undo the procedure is iffy at best. A vasectomy is meant as a one-way operation. If there's any chance you might later get a divorce from the princess-turned-witch you married the first go-round, find a new princess roaming the Eastern Seaboard in search of her prince, and the new princess has an unusual determination to make a baby or two—well, that's something you should have foreseen, or at least considered, before the surgeon put scalpel to skin. So Rick and I have a problem. As for a fix, we have a couple of choices: Reverse the vasectomy or experience the "joy" of sperm extraction.

First things first. Vasectomy reversals are never 100 percent. The exact probability of untying the knots and sewing or gluing the pieces back together depends entirely on whom you ask. Talk to someone who knows and he'll likely tell you that reconnecting A to B is less than 100 percent. That the works get clogged in the process is, say, 30 percent. That some unrelated but lurking problem infringes on the nifty little reversal is, say, 20 percent. I could go on. Put all these probabilities together and the chance of a reversal eventually producing a baby, healthy or otherwise, is about as likely as the kid at Starbucks thoroughly washing his hands every time he returns from the bathroom. It could happen. But let's be honest, it's not likely. That and, even if it did work, it could take months or years to get pregnant.

That leaves sperm extraction and its counterpart, in vitro fertilization. I don't know anybody personally who has gone through IVF, so I plop down at the computer and do my research. Days later it seems, I pull myself away, a bit numbed by all the data, but reasonably convinced this is the route for us. I discover that the University of Maryland performs sperm extraction and IVF procedures; they have a satellite office a short half-hour away. I make an appointment to meet with the doctor, and a week later I am sitting in front of Dr. Griffin, a man with a seven-day old beard, trim hair, and a narrow face. He seldom shows any teeth, but his lips meet in a way that gives the impression he wears a perpetual grin. I tell him Rick and I are in love and we want to make a baby.

"What do we need to do?" I ask.

He talks about the process, making it sound almost breezy, as if we are baking a pie and all it takes from Rick and I is a willingness to follow the recipe. He's either lying or just giving us the Reader's Digest version, the one meant not to scare the hell out of normal, rational people. In vitro, Dr. Griffin tells me, is a procedure that translates literally to mean "within the glass" as in your baby will be conceived, sort of, in a Petri dish.

"Oh," I say, not knowing if this is the right response or if there is a right response.

"Scads of medical experiments are conducted in vitro every year," he says. "It's a simple process, really."

Dr. Griffin opens what looks like a medical chart, though what could be in it that has to do with me I've no idea, since I just arrived. Crib notes, maybe. "We control the ovulatory process using hormones, remove the eggs from your ovaries, and let your husband's sperm fertilize the eggs in a fluid medium."

"We're not married, yet."

"I see," he says and gives me an arch look, examining me now with seriousness.

"We've talked about it," I say.

"Have you?"

"What's next, after the egg is fertilized?"

"The fertilized egg is then transferred to your uterus and, with any luck, you get pregnant."

"You make it sound . . . so clinical."

"Here," he says, and hands me a stack of brochures with glossy photos of giant cells or sperm or eggs in a variety of colors viewed close up through a microscope. "You'll find these helpful."

I go home and tell Rick all about my delightful conversation with Dr. Griffin, and we bat the idea around. This is a big commitment. The procedure is costly and the strain measurable, no matter how much the good doctor tries to make light of it. What goes without saying is that Rick has to suffer through a dispiriting sperm extraction. He doesn't say so, but my guess is most men aren't eager to have a large needle jammed into one of their testicles and a million tiny sperm sucked out.

Okay, everyone on board raise your hand.

Both Rick and I raise our hands.

When Rick tells his fellow doctors and staff at the office about our plans to make a baby, they think he's crazy and don't even try to hide their feelings. On the contrary, they do a pretty good job of talking him out of it. Even his office manager, Sherry, typically a fountain of optimism, can't find a silver lining. "Look," she tells him, "you've been through the hiss and fizzle of a nasty divorce. Now you want more babies. And marriage. I presume there's going to be a marriage. Tell me I'm right, you do plan on marrying her?"

"Her name is Sharon. Is Mr. Hurston ready in room two?"

"Mr. Towers in three," she says. "He's having chest pain, shortness of breath. Better see him first."

"Right."

"Once you get married," Sherry says, "it'll change. Add kids to the picture and you'll be miserable."

"I'll see Towers first. Please let Mr. Hurston know I'll be with him in a few minutes. And Sherry, thanks for the vote of confidence."

"It's what I'm here for."

Even his friends too prudent to say so write us off. They figured the odds we would hit the skids within a year were five to one against. We don't care. We have made our decision and we are moving forward.

At about this time Rick treks north to the Northeast Medical Center clinic in Annapolis and speaks with Dr. Barnes about the sperm extraction. "Nothing could be simpler," Dr. Barnes tells him. A few hours in the hospital under anesthesia, another twenty hours sleeping off the anesthesia at a nearby hotel, and ice packs on his crotch to control the swelling.

Okay, we're in. Before anything gets extracted, Rick and I go through a smattering of tests where a nurse pokes us with needles and drains what seems like buckets of blood. The blood is used to rule out any showstoppers—HIV-1 and 2, hepatitis, and others. We attend orientation class and after some finagling, get our billing clearance. The tab for our little adventure into laboratory baby making comes to an eye-popping 20,000 dollars for the IVF procedure plus another 4,000 dollars for the sperm extraction. We pay a chunk up front and the balance in monthly payments.

The night before Rick's surgery we drive into Baltimore, near the Northeast Medical Center's main teaching hospital, and get a hotel overlooking the harbor. The following morning, the first Wednesday in October, 2005, we show up at the hospital and after a lengthy prep, Rick rolls into surgery around ten-thirty a.m. Dr. Barnes extracts four vials of healthy sperm which means we have four chances at in vitro. Each round requires a vial of sperm. Not that we want four little Ricks or Sharons running round the house, but if it takes a few tries to get pregnant, we're ready. Immediately after the procedure, a technician labels the vials and shuttles them off to the hospital deep freezer where they get stored until the big event. Back at the hotel, I order Rick breakfast and retrieve a bag of ice to keep his testicles from ballooning into grapefruits. We lie around till four, then I drive us home. Even as sore as he is, Rick is a trooper and marches off to work the following day.

The first weekend in November, Rick plans a getaway for the two of us to celebrate my fortieth birthday. His idea is for us to drive north to a little village in far upstate Delaware, spend a couple of days lounging or traipsing through Longwood Gardens, an extravagant conservatory and arboretum. If there's time, I'll sneak in a massage. The trip is more than a birthday present; this time alone is a way of celebrating the start of IFV process, that happy-go-lucky protocol whereby I get the pleasure of jabbing myself with long needles twice a day, injecting all sorts of syrupy-thick fertility meds. The Monday after we return is my own personal IVF D-day, after which there's no turning back.

We reach the inn late afternoon. Our quaint little hotel is in fact a restored nineteenth-century hamlet with twenty-eight guest rooms spread across eleven meticulously restored buildings. We arrive at a veritable microcosm of American history complete with an assortment of spare, well-maintained structures dating back to 1799. Nine of the eleven buildings were original homes for workers at the nearby DuPont Company gunpowder mill. Each suite is richly furnished and has its own privately landscaped courtyards. Oh, and the inn has its own spa with a handful of body rituals to choose from. My favorite (I can tell before even experiencing it) is the Hammam, a seven-step healing massage using mint tea, coffee, olive stones, fresh lemons, orange blossoms, shea butter, and a fig. I learn all this from the young woman who checks us in.

Rick and I meander through the grounds, basically a maze of ornate gardens and cobbled pathways, on our way to our room. Our "room" is closer to a small house, two stories with the bedrooms upstairs and all of it done up in what a little card on the nightstand describes as "Arts and Crafts Period" furniture. This is code language for boxy oak appointments with brown leather cushions, nice enough to look at, and especially comfortable to lounge around on.

Our room sports a marble bath and walk-in shower, a king bed, sturdy wooden four-poster frame, and a gas fireplace. When I come out of the bathroom, a boy is standing just inside the front door, grinning at me awkwardly and holding an antique vase filled with red roses and a bottle of wine. This is Rick's doing, I can tell, a man who leaves nothing to chance. If you want to ensure a romantic weekend, then by all means call ahead and have the inn staff show up with fresh flowers and a bottle of wine the moment you arrive. A man who believes in setting the stage, a habit I find adorable, but also makes me wonder what's next. I don't wait long. Rick ushers the boy out of the room, turns and gives me a hand written note, no doubt another of his little love missives. I look at him and he gives me the little shrug, go on, the shrug says, read it.

I was broken when you met me.
You made me whole.
Your kindness lifted me up,
Your laughter nursed my wounds.
You are my strength when I need it.
You helped me believe in myself again.
The moment we met was magic.
I knew it then.
But what is clear to me now is that the love
And transcendence of our union will only grow with time.
I hope to give you the love and joy you've given me.
I love you, I want to marry and grow old with you.
Will you marry me?

Rick is on one knee next to me, staring up at me. He says the words aloud. "Will you marry me?"

I glance back at the note, at the roses and the wine and the room full of period furniture. "This is unbelievable," I say.

"It is. So what do you say?"

"I do," I say. "I mean, I will. Yes, of course, I will."

He reaches into his pocket, snakes around for several seconds, and emerges with a ring. It has a large circular carat and two smaller baguettes on either side. He holds the ring between his thumb and finger, showing it to me, enticing me to slip my finger through the hole and try it on for size. I ease my finger inside the ring and I cry. It's the best birthday of my life.

I knew it'd happen. I just didn't know when. The weekend getaway, I suspect, was less about celebrating my fortieth and more about catching me off guard. I'm fairly astute at detecting behind-doors maneuverings and motivations, and Rick's natural tendency to sweeten prospects and calm fears. Thus the snappy proposal before I figure it all out and spoil the surprise. We'd talked about marriage, but it was always in a language that seemed far away, as if we were discussing other people's lives. We'd known each other for all of nine months. Not long in the big picture (but an eternity for a forty-year-old woman desperate to make a baby). And even though we'd lived together nearly every day of these last nine months, there were a fair number of life's stories yet to be shared. We didn't, by any means, know all there is to know about each other. I had one or two quasi-embarrassing mysteries yet to tell when the time was right. But we knew enough.

However we weren't the only participants in this dance. Rick's kids hadn't taken to the idea of us as a team. Or it's possible Rick's ex had put her own brand of worries and contingencies in place, stoking the kids with bad vibes and hints that the likelihood of negative outcomes were just over the horizon. "Watch out," the ex seemed to say, "should their little fling grow into something more permanent."

Rough doesn't come close to describing my relationship with Rick's children. My sweet left-brain-thinking, super logical fiancé has this crazy notion that pretending we are chaste as Victorian virgins will make everyone happy, including his kids. Basically, we lie. We pretend we aren't living together, aren't trying our hardest to make babies, and aren't really in love. As far as Ashley and Connor are concerned, their father and I are a couple of somewhat-distant adults who occasionally meet for a glass of Chardonnay and polite dinner conversation and who haven't already sunk our claws into each other and are now holding on for dear life. Rick doesn't want to spill the beans about us living together for fear the ex will do something nasty and get her shyster working overtime to make legal trouble. In practical terms, this means a lot of driving. On the weekends that Rick gets custody of his children, we drive in separate cars from Seaford to the condo where Rick and the kids meet up and spend time together. In keeping with our friends-but-not-much-more storyline, I am invited for dinner but not to stay over. So after clearing the table and washing dishes, I kiss Rick on the cheek like any nervous high schooler, say my goodbyes to a less than enthusiastic threesome of teens, and climb in my car for the hour drive north to our home in Delaware. The whole thing is slightly ridiculous and extremely aggravating, at least to me.

On those occasions when he and I do discuss the unfolding charade (mostly me complaining and Rick soothing me until I purr), neither of us can come up with any legal basis for his fear of retribution. Nonetheless, my man wants to cover all his bases. "Why provoke a fight if you can avoid it, right?" he asks.

"Okay, okay. I give," I say.

So I reluctantly cave to the idea—our little secret can wait until we are officially married. After that, enough with the charade already.

Chapter Five

In Vitro

. . . .

Dr. Griffin's office is on the fifth floor of the Northeast Medical Center. I'd met with him in September at his clinic in Salisbury, but this is my first visit to his office in Baltimore. In the waiting area several couples slouch in uncomfortable chairs, looking gloomy, as if silently rehearsing questions to buttonhole the doctor, and generally passing the long morning in silence. The women frown. The men frown too, but you can tell it takes more effort, a man's way of demonstrating that he cares, that he's on your side and promises to stick it out, though in truth he'd rather be at work returning e-mails or in his car with the music cranked or chasing a dimpled white ball across acres of neatly mowed grass. Let's face it, he'd rather be anyplace but here.

I glance around the room. The woman across from me is looking up and off to the right like some uninspired saint, her hair shooting off in several directions at once, either the latest style and thus super cool, or the result of not giving a hoot what she looks like for these Monday morning visits to the good Dr. Griffin. I feel like she looks, confused and awkward. I'm all alone. Rick is out earning a living checking hearts for clogged plumbing or leaky valves or whatever it is he checks for. That, and I'm the oldest woman in the room by ten years. I feel about a hundred. In the corner, I spot a slim woman in a plaid dress and scoop neckline who looks fifteen. She sees me staring and smiles, then lets the smile fade and turns away.

A cute, bubbly, blonde nurse pops out of a door and calls my name and I stand; she touches me on the arm and immediately I feel better. A simple touch, even from a stranger, is better than the torture of warding off the negative atmosphere of a room full of frowning people.

"I'm Sonya," she says. "Don't worry about a thing, I'll—"

"I want this so badly," I blurt out.

"I know," she says without so much as a hitch in her voice.

Sonya makes me feel at home. She does this sort of thing every day of the week and hearing her reassuring voice puts me at ease. "Excited to begin your IVF cycle?"

"Nervous," I say.

"Don't be. It's fun, you'll see."

I know it's a big fat fib, but I like her all the more for saying it.

She shuttles me to a small office where Dr. Griffin is waiting. He tilts his head forward, looking over the top of his glasses, says something about the weather I instantly forget and before I realize it Sonya is tugging on my sleeve. Meeting over. She guides me to another room painted a faded olive green. The walls are filled with photos of hilariously energetic children in a range of poses. Some are doe-eyed. Others are all baby teeth and squinting eyes. The moms mostly look down at their babies with dreamy stares and immediately I want one of my own. I don't care if he's a he or a she, thin cheeked or pudding-faced, pink or some other color. I just want one. I've reached that indistinct but critical point in life where I know what I want, where most of the things I thought I'd want at forty have suddenly vanished, and I'm left doing the one thing I feel strongest about—sitting here on a small plastic chair in a tiny room full of baby pictures, slightly disoriented, listening to a kind-hearted woman try her best to minimize my pain while giving me the truth as she knows it. I'm ready to begin my trial by fire.

"What's next?" I ask.

"We'll start you on a cycle of fertility medications to stimulate egg production. You'll take the meds at home and if everything works as it should, you'll produce several eggs." Sonya sets her checklist on the narrow counter top. "It's all right," she says as if she understands me, as if she knows what I'm thinking, which is can't we just skip this part, pass Go, and begin the pregnancy already. "Your emotions, I'm afraid, are likely to get away from you at times."

"I'm already there."

"It will get a lot worse," she says, a warm hand on my knee.

"Don't feel you have to sugarcoat it."

"Most women put on a few pounds. The medications and hormones can do that."

"I hate needles."

"Not even doctors like needles."

"But I get a baby at the end of all this?"

"At your age," here Sonya checks here chart to verify that I'm what, like nearly eighty, "wow, okay, like I said we're going to do our best."

"You're not offering a guarantee?"

"Women do get pregnant at your age. It happens."

"Anything else I should know?"

"If you mean side effects, well, you might experience hot flashes and mood swings. I mentioned that, didn't I? Headaches. A lot of women get a nasty rash around the injection site."

"The injection site?" I ask.

"Where you give yourself the shots."

"With needles, you mean?"

"There's also a chance of multiple pregnancy." She smiles at me. "Twins or triplets. It happens."

Sonya hands me a prescription for the fertility medications and several sheets of paper that outline my IVF protocol. On day one of my period, I call and chat with Sonya. Day two, I begin hormonal tests. Day three, I slap on a birth control patch and leave it in place until instructed otherwise. Day four, I do blood work and drop off a urine sample. Day five, I spread my legs and think of pleasant worthwhile purposes while Dr. Griffin gives me a pre-Lupron transvaginal ultrasound. Day six is the big day, the day I begin the fertility meds. This is the day Rick gets to shoot me in the rear and in the tummy with Lupron and a handful of other medications sure to make me crazy and likely, though no guarantees, to produce enough tenacious little egglets to make a baby. Along with Lupron, I take Cetrotide and Novarel and Progesterone (a whopping three-cc dose of oily thick sludge nearly impossible to force through the super-sized needle that comes with it and, without question, the most painful shot in the bunch). Later Repronex and Follistim are added to the queue and probably some others I forgot or intentionally blocked from my memory. It goes like this for the next several weeks, depending on my body's willingness to cooperate.

Every day I get up at five and Rick shoots me with whatever medication the protocol calls for. He talks to me in a kindly voice, which naturally I find extra-irritating.

"Ouch. I thought you were going to numb the area?"

"I did," he says.

"With the stuff, whatever you call it."

"I did."

"What do you call it?"

"A topical."

"The name. What's it called?"

"Emla."

"Well, it doesn't work. Elma. It doesn't work. How's that for an advertising slogan?"

"It works."

"I'm the one getting poked here and it doesn't work." I fan the area with my hand, not really expecting it to do any good but compelled to do something.

"It does what it's supposed to do, which is take the sting out of the shot. It only covers the skin, so once the needle gets past the skin there are other nerves the needle may hit."

"Then you did it wrong, because it still hurts."

"It's a topical."

I yank up my pants and press on the snap. "I know what a topical is. I just don't want it to hurt. Is that too much to ask for?"

"Maybe I should surprise you. Spring it on you while you're asleep."

"You do and I'll put an eye out."

"It's all right, Honey," he says and reaches out to put his arms around me. "Everything's going to be all right."

"I'm late." I turn and stomp away. Sonya was only half right. The meds don't make me crazy. They make me a raving lunatic, a woman without all rational thought, hypersensitive to needles and overly consoling fiancés, a woman who has willingly agreed to sit still and allow herself to play the part of a human pin cushion. This is no way to begin the day, but for me it becomes habit. Wake, shower, get stuck with needles, argue with fiancé, who by the way has several aggravating foibles I never noticed without the aid of fertility drugs, and then trek off to the hospital to be poked and prodded some more.

I climb into Rick's ugly Mountaineer, a car I positively loathe and would pay thousands to have stolen the moment I turn my back. I drive the monster at my fiancé's rational suggestion that we not put too many miles on the car I love, a light-blue convertible Mercedes. (He may have actually hypnotized me into believing this was a good idea.) So here I am, medicated, neurotic, driving a car I detest and the car knows it. On one trip into Baltimore I park, legally mind you, and a city snowplow scrapes the entire side of the Mountaineer and the four cars parked ahead of me. After we get the beast patched up and painted, I'm hit from behind while sitting at a red light. Isn't a car supposed to be a safe haven, an ordinary and predictable reinforced metal box meant to protect you from a hazardous world? Only the world, it seems, hates this car as much as I do. Nonetheless, I climb aboard and drive two hours through heavy traffic into Baltimore, take a wrong turn or two, park, walk on swollen feet into the lobby of the Northeast Medical Center, take the elevator to the fifth floor, and march into the doctor's office by seven a.m. I meet with Sonya, who verifies that everything is on track and on schedule.

"Next week," she says, "we'll see you again next week. Okay, everything else looks good. All done."

For my two-hour one-way drive, I get all of thirteen words and not especially critical words at that.

On subsequent visits she gives me the skinny on the fertility medications by sharing with me, semi-conspiratorially, that the drugs are intended to get my ovaries working overtime. This I already know. I'm marrying a doctor, I want to shout at her, but don't. I'm in a mood but don't want to alienate my guide for the journey. She checks my estradiol level, takes blood, or has me pee in a cup and sends me on my way.

At home Rick is a calming force, but there's a limit to just how much calm one man can muster. I'm losing it emotionally and even I know it. I look forward to this evening's shot because I feel angry and unloved. And fat. And I want to argue and bicker and scratch at something until its insides are showing or until I feel better, whichever comes first. Rick and I are in our bedroom, me half lying on the bed on top of my favorite duvet made of a linen-cotton blend rendered in sun-drenched shades of gold, green, and blue. Ours is a bedroom of creamy wood trim, deep carpets, and halftone lighting. Rick stands next to the nightstand, a syringe in one hand and a small vial of something oily and viscous in the other. He is tall and handsome and getting on my nerves, the anticipation of one more tiny sliver of steel piercing my skin makes me involuntarily flinch.

"Lie on the bed, here," Rick says. He points the syringe where he wants me, in a place with good light.

I tug down my pants and show him the spot, now red as a wine stain. "You're thinking of her, I can tell."

"Who?" he says.

"You know who." This is me picking a fight. I turn my head away and shift my hips without knowing. Or did I?

"Hold still."

"That woman, the one before me."

"Hold still."

"Admit it. You're thinking of her."

"My ex-wife? I can promise you I'm not thinking of my ex."

He puts one hand on my behind and I grit my teeth, waiting. "The other woman," I say. "The one with the chin. Don't pretend you don't know who we're talking about. Is that the kind of woman you want? Is it?"

"Sharon, honey. Just hold still. I'll be done here in a minute."

"You won't even talk about her. Why, because she gained all that weight. Is that it, a woman gains some weight, she gets an extra chin, or two, and you, what, you walk away? Ouch."

"Done. First, she gained a few pounds, is all. Second, I didn't walk away because she was overweight. I got swindled. I don't like to date women who swindle me. Is that so unreasonable?"

"That hurt." I rub the spot with the tips of my fingers, feeling for anything that might not be right. "I saw the picture."

"It's not enough this woman took me for over a half a million dollars in a bad real estate deal? Now you even think of her, dig up an old photo, anything, and I have to explain myself?"

"I can't sit," I say.

"Roll the other way."

"I'm having one of those nights," I say.

"Like I don't know?"

The strongest feeling I have now is that something isn't right and I don't know what that something is.

"Days of shots," Rick says fiddling with his needles and medications, "you think I can't see it coming?"

"One of those nights where the pain never goes away."

"It's a shot, honey. It goes away."

"Not that pain. The other."

"What?"

"I never told you this. . ."

"What?"

"A man who dates a woman like that, he could date anyone. How do you think that makes me feel?"

"It was a bad photo. The angle would have made anyone look bad. The photographer must have been drinking."

"I found another photo today. Not of you and her, but just her."

"You found it?"

"In a photo album way in the back of the closet under the books. It was hiding there, but I found it."

"My little spy," he says.

"A few pounds?"

"Fifteen or twenty, I think it was. She never said."

I roll on my back and stare at the ceiling, the creamy wooden trim of the ceiling. "I'm gaining weight."

"You're having a baby."

"Not yet I'm not."

I am gaining weight. One pound, three pounds. A couple of weeks into the cycle, I've put on six pounds. A couple of weeks later, I'm expanding at a near-constant rate. Each morning I experience the joy of sifting through my clothes. This fits. This doesn't. This used to fit. This will never fit again. I'm not thinking straight, I know that, but knowing it doesn't make me feel any better. Then a thought hits me. What if I never stop gaining weight? Is that even possible? So what if it isn't? It could still happen. This is how women on fertility meds think. It's how their brains work, which is to say, not working so well.

I stand there in the middle of my glorious walk-in closet and weep. I'm miserable. This morning I opened the fridge, took one peek inside and started bawling. And not for the obvious reason that eating would make me even fatter, but because I couldn't decide what to eat. Choosing a couple of eggs over, say, half a grapefruit or a carton of yogurt or a glass of orange juice was a monumental undertaking. I long for one of those brains capable of cranking through seven gazillion possible alternatives, the kind chess grandmasters with thick eyebrows and large ears take for granted. Since starting on the fertility drugs, my cognitive processes are either running overtime or shut down. And I've no way of knowing which is which. I stood there with the stainless steel handle of the fridge firmly in hand, gaping at all my choices, seriously considering making a pros and cons list. I changed my mind, opting for the first-thing-to-catch-my-eye approach, but before anything catches my eye, I decided to flip a coin. Only I don't have a coin on me and finding one was way too much effort. Instead, I began to cry. I let go of the handle and watched the fridge door glide closed, I sobbed all the harder when I heard that familiar soft sucking noise the door makes when it closes tight.

There are mornings Rick isn't home, having left for the office or hospital at an ungodly hour, and I give myself the shot. I don't cry or hesitate or even wince. This from the woman who hates needles. Over the past several weeks I've changed, morphed into another woman, stronger in some ways, a person who pokes herself with large needles in exchange for the promise of a worthwhile outcome. Each time I penetrate the skin, a little blotchy rash forms around the spot. I stare at the redness as if it's not really my skin or my leg or my body, but some other person's body and leg and rash. I think that person should do something about the rash before it gets any worse. I think that person should take better care of herself, exercise, and maybe drop a few pounds. I think that person is probably stubborn as a donkey and unwilling to admit she needs a little help, or at a minimum some kindly advice on how to make ugly rashes disappear. Worse, the rash itches throughout the day and only stops itching moments before I give myself another shot. Then the itching begins all over again.

I do the shot thing for a couple of weeks or more, then return to Dr. Griffin's office for a nifty little transvaginal ultrasound. The black and white fuzzy image on the screen shows that I'm ready, there are enough eggs, that the chances of extracting several healthy eggs are better than average. Dr. Griffin says to Sonya, "All right, schedule the HCG and egg retrieval. We're done here."

He scoots out of the small exam room. On the wall behind where Dr. Griffin had just standing, I see the large face of a baby staring back at me. It's a boy with dark eyes and an unusually square face. Sonya moves in front of the photo, directly in front of me. "This is it," she says. She leans over the narrow counter and scribbles on a piece of light green paper. She presses hard, carving the letters into the page. Her wrist and arm move at a furious pace in jerky diagonal motions. The baby watches me, accepting, inquisitive. I get dressed and find that moving my shoulders and neck has wakened an all-over achiness. Sonya straightens, hands me the piece of paper. On it she's written more instructions. Tonight I will stick myself and inject hefty doses of Profasi, Novarel, and Ovidrel. She lists the exact date and time for the HCG injection as well as my stimulation meds and Lupron.

"Follow the schedule," she says. "Really, this is really important that you stick to the schedule."

"Tell me again what HCG is?"

"Human chorionic gonadotropin."

"What it does, I mean."

"It helps maintain progesterone production."

"I have an ache. Oh boy do I have an ache."

"I know about the ache. The ache is good. Everything is good. Follow the schedule. Please." She reaches out and touches me on the arm and I feel better. A trick they teach you in nursing school—acknowledge the pain, tell them the pain is good, and offer a touch on the arm or knee or back or hand or wherever that magic place is, that bull's-eye drawn in invisible ink only nurses and lovers can read.

"If I don't," I say, moody and combative, "if I forget or I'm late, what happens then?"

"You won't forget."

"If I do, what then?"

She squeezes my arm, giving me a double dollop of kindness. "No one ever forgets their last shot."

Chapter Six

Egg Retrieval Day

....

December 9, 2005, is egg retrieval day. It's a Friday and I love
Fridays. It's a stroke of good luck that my doctor will have a
go at plucking my eggs on a day I find downright magical.
The actual plucking takes place on the seventh floor of the Northeast
Medical Center. The morning of the big show, I get up at three a.m. and
wake Rick, who worked late last night at the hospital, dragged himself
home, plopped into bed, for an hour or so before I start elbowing him to
get going. I load my duffle into the car, open the garage door, crank the
motor and the cumbersome SUV rattles to life. It's dark out. Rick is beat
and his eyes are puffy, a sure sign he needs sleep and is in no mood for a
chatty conversation about what's coming up.

Inside the SUV, the temperature hovers around freezing so I ratchet
the heater knob up to scorch. It's noisy and the steering wheel is an ice
cube. The windows, front and back, are already fogged, and I fiddle with
the defrost lever which does nothing as far as I can tell. Did I mention
that I hate this car? I ask Rick if he could stop breathing, just until the
windows clear. I flash him a glowing smile, but he doesn't bother to look
at me. Instead gives me a weather report. "We are smack in the middle of

the biggest snowstorm in decades," he says. While I slept, a winter storm had apparently dumped a foot and a half of snow across parts of New England. Our slumberous lower Delaware has gotten more white stuff in a couple of days than it got all last year. We haven't left the cozy comfort of the garage and already I feel this is a bad idea, Friday or no Friday. I turn on the lights and back out of the garage and hear the soft crunchy sounds of tires on ice and snow. I pull onto River Drive, swing out of Cedar Shores and hang a left on Atlantic Road. I flip on my brights. It doesn't look too bad. It's windy and cold out and there's plenty of snow everywhere, but some kind soul has pushed most of it to the side of the road. My fingers are turning blue from a combination of cold and the fear that if I let go of the wheel, if I ease too far left or right, the tires could catch a block of ice and pull me off into the gray-black ditch. All around me the forest is blanketed in patches of white glowing in the moonlight. The cypress trees are struggling, their branches heavy with ice and snow, giving the trees a weighty presence I hadn't noticed before. Twenty minutes into the trip we merge onto Route 404 where the landscape changes to fields of turned earth in neat rows and a layer of untouched snow smoothing over the furrows.

"Tell me again," I say.

Rick stares resolutely ahead, watching the giant flakes glow in the headlights as clean and evenly spaced as movie snow shot out of an industrial snow blower. "It's a minor surgery," he grumbles, but he knows what I want to hear. He slouches and lets his body go all loose-jointed and leans his head on the plastic next to the foggy window. He's thinking seriously about getting some sleep, but hasn't fully committed to the idea. "Really, it's nothing to worry about."

"I know, but I so much want this to work. I can't help but worry."

"It's all antibiotics and anesthesia," Rick says. "Dr. Griffin has done this hundreds of times."

"I know, it's not the surgery, it's just… I'm scared."

A car comes at me in the opposite direction and flashes its brights. I flip the little knob, turning my lights back to what, super dim? Now

I can't see a thing. The highway in front of me has all but vanished into the darkness. It takes several seconds for my eyes to adjust and when they do, I slow the big SUV and grip the wheel even tighter. "Tell me again."

"I'm sure he's done this thousands of times, but it's really not my area."

My nose is running and I reach into my purse beside me and sift through the contents as if panning for gold, something that drives Rick crazy, me taking my focus off the road, but it's grab a tissue now or let my nose run down the front of my new tweed winter jacket, which isn't happening. "Just tell me again."

So he shuts his eyes, lets himself sink into his seat and tells me about the ultrasound-guided needle that pierces the vaginal wall and sucks out the eggs. I swerve to miss a couple of snow covered orange cones in the road.

"What was that about?" he says, looking up, but he doesn't see the cones.

"Nothing, go on."

The needle, he tells me, punctures the follicle, the fluid filled sac that holds the eggs, and then the doc sucks out the fluid and eggs. He doesn't even mention the pain. This I have to find out about on the Internet where plenty of post-egg-retrieval women happily tell me and anyone who can read that the fun isn't over once you've given up the goods. Some women hurt, even with the anesthesia. After, lots of women experience fatigue and pelvic soreness.

"Can we slow down?" Rick says.

"You sleep, I'll drive," I say, but he's got a point and I do slow to avoid plowing into the puny Honda in front of me.

"Go easy," he says. "Just a tap on the breaks."

"Go on, get some sleep," I say, which naturally brings him wide awake, sitting upright in his seat, leaning forward, watching the traffic and gauging the thickness and slickness of the ice. We skate around Denton and Queen Anne without incident and onto Route 50 west where everyone is driving way faster than reasonable even if the road has recently been cleared of icebergs. It's now coming down in flakes the size of maple leaves, so fluffy, full, and fast I can't see the end of the hood. Rick and I talk about the Chesapeake Bay Bridge, still almost an hour ahead of us. "They won't close it," I say.

"It's coming down hard," he says.

"They won't. They can't. Too many people need to get across."

"They'll close it if they need to."

"And what, strand us?"

"Or save our lives."

I turn and look at him steadily, and what this stare means is that I'm in no mood for a logical give and take on saving lives, mine or anyone else's. If I don't make it to the hospital today, this morning, I've missed my window of opportunity, egg-wise. It's this day, this morning, right now, or I go through the cycle again—the wide-legged exams and belly shots and losing my mind. There's no way I'm not getting across that bridge, closed or otherwise, I will swim the bay and crawl into Baltimore on all fours if that's what it takes. I flip on the radio and the morning DJs are carrying on about the storm. Lightning dances across the sky, claps of thunder boom overhead, and a wet, sticky snow descends at a rate of two inches an hour. All the schools are closed but that doesn't keep the nasally voiced guy from listing each and every school by name. As for government employees, it's code red, whatever that means. Highway 50 is getting worse, icier and churned up at the same time. The snow-pushers are out in force, giant dump trucks with bright yellow plows nudging the gathering snow off to the side of the road. The temperature is dropping and the freshly ploughed snow re-freezes into rock-hard clumps I avoid if possible and sometimes just grip the wheel and wait for the bump. Visibility has vanished. I'm stressed, imagining the worst of my upcoming little procedure. My nose runs and I've dropped my tissue somewhere on the wet floorboard. Then from nowhere a question rockets through my mind. *Someone tell me again why I'm making a baby in a test tube?*

I yank the SUV to the side of the road and brake hard. "I can't take it."

"Is everything all right?"

"I hate this car." I don't look at Rick because I'm this close to crying.

"Sharon, honey."

"Please, you drive. I'll be okay."

We pull over and he takes over. We slog into Kent Island, pass the marina and ease onto the concrete and steel of the Chesapeake Bay Bridge—not closed—then onto I-97 north into Baltimore.

By the time we pull into the hospital parking lot it's six-thirty a.m. and still dark as mud and achingly cold. I'm frozen, tired, and frazzled from the drive. Rick, on the other hand, is wide awake, even chipper now that we're off the road far from all the other crazies without the good sense to stay home in such weather.

I rub my hands together, reach for my purse and wipe my nose with a soggy tissue. I do a face check in the rearview mirror. I look nervous, but all right. "Okay," I say. "Let's do this."

We slog up to the seventh floor and march over to labor and delivery. I tell the girl at the desk who I am and why I'm here. She points to a seat in the waiting room. The waiting room is done up in a purplish flower motif with rows of soft cushioned chairs, most of them filled with pregnant women and red-eyed hubbies. I hear babies crying off in the distance. I want to ask if I can hold one and rock him or her and sort of get a head start on mothering. I read somewhere that mothers intuitively hold their babies on their left arm. This makes them turn left to look into the baby's face. And turning left triggers the right side of the brain, the part with all the good stuff, empathy and pattern recognition that can tell what a baby wants by the wrinkles in his face, the way his eyes scrunch up and his lips part, and the little micro expressions of love.

We sit and right away my back aches, probably from the massive dose of HCG that Rick jammed into my bottom precisely thirty-four hours ago, per instructions. Besides stimulating the ovaries to produce and release eggs, HCG hormone can generate a spectacular body ache. My jolt of human chorionic gonadotropin resulted in a double whammy, stimulation and ache, one that spreads across my shoulders, radiates down my spine and ends somewhere about ten inches past my toes.

On top of it, I'm starved. My instructions said not to eat a bite after midnight, and though I can typically go foodless for more than six, seven hours, the very prohibition makes me hungry, starved, famished. I want nothing more than a big plate of pan-roasted halibut with risotto and artichoke hearts. No, make that lobster spaghetti with spicy tomato sauce and a side of roasted fennel.

The girl at the desk calls my name and I stand and hug Rick and say goodbye like one of those love stories where someone, usually the man, stands on a train platform in some exotic European city and hugs his lover who cries and the man boards the train anyway. A nurse leads me to a room with a curtain surrounding a bed and I undress and put on a hospital gown and crawl into the bed. This is pre-op and I'm lying there protected by this flimsy curtain and on the other side of the curtain is another woman lying in bed waiting for the same thing. I hear voices and I know there are three of us. Maybe more. Waiting.

I hear some clanking and rubber wheels and one of the women is wheeled away. Sometime later the other woman is taken, silently, calmly, all in a day's work. Finally, a nurse comes and takes blood and inserts an IV into the back of my left hand. The nurse wheels me into the operating room where it's painfully bright and I scoot onto a table and a man asks me to count backwards from one hundred and before I reach, well, I can't remember, I'm out.

I'm barely awake from the anesthesia, laying flat on my back in post-op and already praying that the doctor found enough eggs. Through the flimsy dull blue curtain surrounding my bed on wheels I hear other women on both sides of me and more women next to them. I hear the calming words of a nurse occasionally punctuated by a male voice I take for the doctor, speaking in crisp declarative sentences.

"Good news," doc says.

"Oh?" a woman says.

"We got what we needed. Several eggs of good quality."

"Thank heaven for that."

I'm happy for that woman. The news isn't guaranteed to be good. Well before arriving this morning, I'd been prepped for the other kind. The doctor might tweeze out as many as sixteen feisty eggs and everyone is ecstatic, Sonya told me, then over the next several hours all but two or three can wither and die. "Let's think positive," Sonya said to me, though what she was really saying was, "Let's not get ahead of ourselves. Let's just take it one step at a time and see what we see and go from there."

"Okay," I told her. "One step at a time it is."

I'm still groggy and fall back asleep. At some point I hear the doctor saying he's sorry. He retrieved eggs, he says, but they were all defective, unusable. He's truly, truly sorry. I open my eyes and look around. No one's there. At first I think it was a dream, then I hear the woman behind the curtain begin to sob and I know it's not. I feel bad for her and at the same time hope things go a little better for me.

The real Dr. Griffin arrives carrying a chart, head down as if prepping himself to deliver the bad news. "How do you feel?"

"All I'm thinking about is the eggs."

He reaches over and lifts my wrist, I presume taking my pulse—and makes a note in the chart. "Any pain, grogginess?" he asks, stalling.

"You did get some eggs. Am I right?"

"Yes, of course," he says.

"How many?"

"Six eggs total. No As or Bs, I'm afraid."

"No As or Bs?"

"Mostly Cs," he says and looks puzzled for the first time, which naturally throws me because I've no idea what he could be puzzled about.

"Cs are good," I say with all the confidence of a freshmen one quiz away from flunking out.

"And a couple of Es."

"But you got four good eggs, is that what you're saying? The six minus the two that's, what, four good eggs? They are good, right? I mean, good enough, mature, whatever term it is you use."

"Precisely," he says as I stare up at his tough, firm lips. He's a man used to doing most of the talking even if what he actually says makes little sense like what's happening right now. For the first time I wonder where my cardiologist fiancé is hiding and wish he were here to translate. It's possible I am a tad groggy and think about saying so when Dr. Griffin says, "If there's nothing else, I have other patients to attend to," and he's off.

From here things are out of my hands. If all goes well, what's supposed to happen is this. The eggs, my eggs, are scooped out of me and immediately marched over to the lab where a sharp-eyed embryologist has a close-up look under a microscope, grades each egg for maturity (presumably already done) and slips the juicy dish into a nearby incubator. The maturity of an egg is critical because it determines when the sperm will be added. Introduce the egg and sperm too early and they might stare lovingly at each other from across the Petri dish, but chances of any real romance taking place is all but nil. Too late and both wither and die. Timing is everything. In most cases, insemination takes place a couple of hours after retrieval. A lab tech squirts a milliliter of Rick's freshly unfrozen and presumably still sticky sperm alongside each of my eggs, each in its own hyper clean dish, and plops each dish back into an incubator. The incubator is kept at a constant temperature designed to fool the egg/sperm combo into thinking they met somewhere in the fallopian tube. They fall in love and merge into a healthy embryo. Hours later the tech ambles in and checks to see how many eggs have fertilized. No matter how good the egg and sperm may look under the scope, anything can happen. Deep down, I am prepared for the worst.

The next day, Sonya calls. All four of my eggs fertilized. Congratulations, she says. The call brings in a welcome, freeing moment, a space to breathe without anxiety. I've crossed a hurdle, a major milestone on my way to making a baby. If I could reach through the phone I'd give

Sonya a big kiss. I'd even plant one on the embryologist in the lab for keeping an eye on my infant embryos snug in their Petri dishes, where they divide and divide and divide.

Two days later, I drive back to Baltimore, take the elevator up seven floors and lay on a table for the embryo transfer, a process of delicately placing the embryos back into my uterus.

The embryo transfer is, without question, the most humiliating experience of my life. This from a woman who has done some spectacularly humiliating things, most of which I choose not to share. I'm wheeled back into the operating room, moved to a table and get my legs strapped into a contraption with all my privates clearly visible, one leg here and the other way over there in a position that could only feel natural to an aerobics instructor or yoga guru. Surrounding me at the bottom of the operating table is an army of green clad medical types standing there puzzling over at the scene before them. What makes the experience even worse is that I'm wide awake, taking it all in one agonizing second after another, staring up at the overly bright lights and wishing it were all over with.

A man's voice I recognize as Dr. Griffin says, "How are we feeling?"

"Fine," I say, meaning that I feel just about how I imagine most women feel while laying here spread eagled and half naked. How he's feeling, if that's whom he means by "we," I have no idea.

"Well now, the embryo transfer procedure is quite simple. No anesthetic, but you may feel a bit of discomfort." He says this with his head between my legs. Two other nurses, I suppose, are down there, heads lowered, everyone with a good view of the show. "I'm going to expose the cervix and clean the area with sterile water." Here he waits for a beat, giving me time to respond.

"Fine."

"I'll take the embryos suspended in a drop of culture and load them into the transfer catheter." He pauses and holds up the catheter for me to see, a long white and blue tube with a syringe on one end. "And then gently guide the tip of the catheter through the vagina and cervix and deposit the embryos into the uterine cavity."

"I'm okay if we just get on with it."

"After the catheter is removed, I'll hand it over to the embryologist here who will check to ensure that no embryos remain. If I do my job correctly, implantation will begin in three to four days."

I'm sure Dr. Griffin is a swell guy, someone Rick and I would happily share a glass of wine with or a tall glass of ink-dark beer or whatever IVF docs drink when they aren't hands on, but this isn't then, and I'm ready to get things moving. Dr. Griffin stands and begins to speak. I hold up my hand, palm forward, a sign that says "Please, no more talk. I can't take it." The good doctor, an astute reader of patient signs, stops talking, nods at one of the others, resumes his place between my spread legs and gets to it.

Rick and I have to wait two weeks to see if any of the embryos took. Anyone who's ever been through IVF knows how hard it is to sit around and do nothing while your body decides if it's willing to give the go-ahead for a baby. On day fourteen, I return to the doctor's office for a blood test, drive two hours home, stare out the back window at the Nanticoke River and wait. That afternoon I get a call from Sonya. She tells me I have a high level of beta HCG, a hormone produced by the embryo and a sign all is going according to plan. I return to the office three days later, praying my beta level has risen. It has. I'm pregnant. In fact, my beta has shot up so fast, it's likely, Sonya says, I'm in for a surprise, though she's playing coy and won't give it up. On my next visit Dr. Griffin makes it official. I'm five weeks pregnant. "Oh," he says, "did I mention you're having twins?"

Chapter Seven

Married and Pregnant

···

O n February 12, 2006—our one year anniversary and eleven weeks into the pregnancy it's time for Rick and me to tie the knot. I've done the church thing before and am not interested in a repeat performance. Ditto for Rick. We want a nontraditional wedding, though neither of us has any idea what that means. We also have no intention of dragging his kids along. We haven't even told them that I, we, are pregnant. Our motto, at least with regard to Matthew, Ashley and Connor, is no rocking the boat until after the wedding.

We decide on Las Vegas and fly out a couple of days early, check in at the Bellagio, and get tickets to one of the Cirque du Soleil shows. The day after the show, we get up early and schlep downtown to get our marriage certificate where, once we find the place, we fill out a lengthy Affidavit of Application for a Marriage License, prove up our age and show our social security cards. No blood test. No waiting period.

Prior to settling on Las Vegas, I Google dozens of wedding locations. I look through the top ten—Hawaii, New York City, San Francisco, Miami, Las Vegas, New Orleans, Aspen, Lake Tahoe, Martha's Vineyard,

Napa Valley—and for whatever reason circled Las Vegas, the marriage capital of the world. We want unusual and private, even remote, if we can get it.

One option is the Venetian Hotel and Casino which comes with a one night stay in the wedding suite, an hour in the Venezia Tower chapel, a photo, bottle of Moet champagne, and a glide down the Grand Canal in a low-slung, semi-authentic gondola all for a couple of thousand dollars.

"That's kind of creepy," Rick says when I mention the idea. "Strangers standing around staring as you float by."

"There's always the Elvis wedding chapel," I say.

"I will if you will."

"It comes with two pair of Elvis sunglasses."

"Does Elvis sing?"

"Three songs."

"What about the Valley of Fire?" I say. I shuffle through all the paperwork I'd printed from the Internet and find what I'm looking for. "Let's see. Valley of Fire State Park located in the lovely Mojave Desert. Home of brilliant sandstone formations created some 150 million years ago by wind and water erosion."

"Are you serious?"

"About which part?" The two of us are standing in the kitchen, Rick with one hand on the open refrigerator door, and me in front of the high counter. "See for yourself." I wave a photo at him, a giant red-orange rock, the texture of fine grit sandpaper, with an irregular hole in the middle tall enough to drive through.

"The movie *Star Trek: Generations* was filmed there."

"That's ten years old."

"Older."

"I liked that movie."

"So what do you think?"

"What do *you* think?"

I think it sounds different and private and more or less exactly what we want.

The whole shebang is supposed to be just the two of us. In the end, my parents raise such a stink, we say, "Why not? Please join us," and they do. We have a nice couple of days before they arrive. On the day of the wedding, Rick arranges for a limo and we pile in and ride out to the park, about an hour outside of Las Vegas. Once we get close, the red rocks are like wow, way cooler than I imagined. Private doesn't begin to describe our little wedding milieu. The place is vacant, empty of hikers and half-drunken gamblers and onlookers of any kind. Nothing but moody, silent boulders with a primal attraction hard to explain. It's perfect.

We meet the minister, a short, heavyset black man with an Al Sharpton look to him, a camera man with a digital camera and larger video camera strung around his neck. The four of us chat for less than eight seconds. The minister points to a path and starts walking. We follow with my parents bringing up the rear, and come to a jutting section of rusty-orange mini-mountain that forms a massive and symmetrical rock arch. I can't for the life of me imagine a more beautiful and fitting place for the ceremony. A part of the rock flattens out into a platform of sorts about a dozen feet above ground. Rick and I begin the climb, the stones shifting in several directions at once. Rick is wearing a new black suit and polished shoes, and I'm in a satin, ankle- length evening gown that catches and grabs at the sandstone. Twice I step on my dress, teetering bent-kneed ready to tumble headfirst off our sweet matrimonial cliff. My polite fiancé keeps me plumb, occasionally pushing me in the rear, propping me up with his big strong hands, and keeping the twins and me from losing it before we even get hitched. We make it, both of us standing tall in front of the arch, the blue sky all around. I lean into Rick and say, "I feel fat."

"You look lovely," he whispers.

"Eleven weeks," I say. "All of it right here." I pat my belly.

"Twins." He reaches over to pat my belly and I push his hand away. I stare down at my stomach. "Can you tell?"

"A little midriffy, is all. You're beautiful. I love you."

This, of course, is what I want to hear. "Okay," I say to the minister. "We're ready."

The entire ceremony takes seven minutes, less if you subtract the chitchat when we arrived. Climbing back down takes ages, like forty-five minutes at least, both of us moving an inch at a time. Me holding a bouquet of light orange flowers in one hand and tugging at my gown to keep the hem from getting in the way with the other. If simple is your wish, the Valley of Fire State Park is a wish made real.

In the limo on the way back to town, Rick pops a bottle of champagne to share with my parents—I can't drink—and the three of them have a gay old time.

Back home it seems my life is spent on the road. I leave early and arrive home late. When I have to shoehorn in doctor visits and lab work in Baltimore, I get up even earlier and arrive home even later. For all the effort, things only get worse. My bosses acted annoyed when I told them about my engagement, and are even more visibly so after I tell them about my marriage to Rick, as if formalizing our couple hood might cut into my productivity. As a single girl, I'm apparently considered pliable. As a married woman and pregnant, I'm, what? Less dedicated? Nonetheless my bosses and I are very good at our respective trades. I make connections and sell independent agents on using our X Insurance Services. But unfortunately my two "superiors" have become incredibly creative at explaining, often acting breathless in the telling, how each new client is connected to them and thus, no commission is coming my way. Despite this, with hard work I still manage decent earnings.

In March I feel okay, if okay includes tender breasts, fatigue, nausea, backaches, headaches, and a constant urge to pee. And hunger pangs like nothing I'd experienced and never seem to end. Oh, and my nipples have turned a dark, unpleasant blue-purple. And, I experience a little spotting. When I visit with the doctor, he tells me I'm par for the course.

"What about the spotting?" I ask.

"Nothing but a bit of implantation bleeding," he says, while washing his hands at the mini-sink in the exam room. "Spotting, some cramping. All perfectly normal."

"I haven't had any cramping."

"You will."

There is a long silence and I don't know whether to laugh, frown, or gird myself for the cramp I think I can feel working its way down low from back to front. I realize it's just my bladder pressing on something it shouldn't and I have to pee.

"Ok then."

Later in the month, Rick wants to take his two youngest off to Disney World in Orlando. Since the wedding things have changed for the better, so we go, and for entire days it seems the kids are happy and content with the world and their father and his new wife. Ashley, at least, is over the willies that I'm pregnant and transitions nicely into excitement, even joy that we're having a baby, babies.

We bring one of Ashley's friends along, a sweet girl.

"I hope it's a girl," Ashley says to her friend.

"You can name it Joslin," the friend says. "It means just one."

"What about the other one?"

"Oh, right, well—"

We leave Walt Disney World on a positive note, the air thick with optimism and the scent of cotton candy and Mickey-shaped waffles.

Chapter Eight

Something's Not Right

···

My local obstetric/gynecology expert is Dr. Gomez, a nice woman who takes her time with every movement of her slim body and who works with her husband, Dr. Romero, a gynecology/urology specialist and a bit of a superstar in the GYN/Urology world. I meet both at their Delaware office and am struck by how they spoke to each other, not as husband and wife, but as sophisticated Brazilian diplomats perhaps discussing an issue of politics. They are aloof and engaged at the same time, the way only professional actors and foreigners seem to pull off with any panache, and they put on this little display with each other as well as their patients. They have the appearance of people waiting for something better, chins held high, eyes perpetually looking over your shoulder—at what I have no idea. I feel I'm lucky to have latched on to them.

On one of my first visits Dr. Gomez stares intently at the printout of an ultrasound. She says, "The embryos, I see that one implanted very low."

"Low? What does that mean?" I ask.

"You don't know this?" Dr. Gomez shakes her head and looks down at the printout. "From me, this is the first you are hearing of this?"

"I don't think so. I mean, yes, this is the first. In any event, what does that mean?"

"The embryo, this one," she says and points to a speck of dust on the paper in her hand, "it implanted close to the cervix."

"Anatomically low, you mean."

"Yes, yes. I forget you are married to a doctor."

Abruptly, Dr. Romero glides into the exam room, ears perked like a man with supersonic hearing, and takes the printout from his wife. "This one," he says, tapping the piece of paper, "will be a vanishing twin. The embryo will be absorbed." He waves his hands up in the air like a magician. He doesn't say poof, but I hear it anyway.

"And the other?" I ask.

"Oh, fine, fine. Nothing to worry about. Perfectly healthy."

Weeks pass and wouldn't you know it, Dr. Romero is wrong. A man with all the confidence of a senator misses the mark by a wide margin. My vanishing twin never vanishes. Instead, it grows at the same rate as his/her upper sibling, the one pocketed away deep in the uterus where life is good and chances of absorption and poof are all but impossible. I ask Dr. Gomez if this is going to be a problem, you know, both babies growing away, one low, one high.

"Oh, no, no," she says. "All is fine."

I stare up at her smooth brown face and dark eyes, my own face intentionally blank in a move I learned from an old sales pro who taught me that if you quiet your mind, keep your yap shut, and wait long enough, the chances are good that the next words out of your customer's, teacher's, or doctor's mouth will be the truth.

She says, "Everything, it is fine."

As the weeks whiz by, my confidence grows and grows and, well, grows. I can do this. I can do this. I'm making a baby, two babies. I can do this. On a subsequent visit, the doctor hands me a parting gift, a video sonogram of the babies at seventeen weeks, and for whatever reason, I don't watch the video. I can't. I'm afraid I'll kibitz the whole thing, afraid to get myself too attached to the little tikes mounting inside me. If I do watch, I know what I'll see—thin eyebrows, maybe some hair on their oval heads, and eight rubbery limbs.

At nineteen weeks I find out I'm having boys. Both of them. We're well past the halfway point and I'm thinking everything really is fine. I let go a spoonful of anxiety, tomorrow another spoonful. Shortly thereafter, I climb into my car and head up to a hospital in Annapolis to visit a doctor who specializes in level two ultrasounds. At forty, I'm essentially an old maid for a pregnancy. I need extra attention, and doubling up on the ultrasounds is the prescription. Dr. Sutton, a small man with an angular face and skilled fingers, rubs a tiny transducer the shape of a computer mouse across my tummy. The mouse spits out high frequency sound waves that turn into real-time continuous pictures of my babies moving around inside me.

The doctor presses the mouse into my skin and moves it back and forth across my belly. He squints at the monitor and rubs some more.

"It's a bit cold in here," I say.

The doctor glances at me and wipes his forehead with the back of his sleeve. "Just a moment longer." Only a moment takes minutes with more rubbing and more squinting and none of it feels like good news.

"I didn't get a chance to say so, but I have a slight pain right here," I say, and press on my belly down low.

Dr. Sutton doesn't take his eyes off the monitor.

"Like severe cramping, though not really," I say. "More like a shooting pain."

Dr. Sutton lifts the mouse and steps backward away from the monitor and stretches and cranks his head hard left then right, the way a professional wrestler might and makes a low throaty grunt.

"Well?" I say.

"The lower twin is losing amniotic fluid."

"What?"

"The sac surrounding the fetus, the amniotic fluid must be leaking. There could be several causes – a cold, a viral infection. It's too early to tell."

"And the other one?"

"Both boys are fine."

I move to get up and reach for my sweater because some energy conscious zealot has cranked the thermostat down to sub zero.

"Please remain where you are. I'll be right back." He tries to grin, but this is a man unaccustomed to smiling and it comes off as an expression not entirely comforting. And like that, he marches out the door leaving me on my back, belly bared, and worried silly.

My first impulse is to call Rick. I get him on the phone and shout at him to do something. It doesn't matter that he's two hours away and has only a second of free time between patients—some nearly as hysterical as I am—and they too need his full attention. Rick tries to calm me but I'm way past calming.

"Isn't there something you can do?" I say.

"I know about hearts, honey. This isn't a heart problem."

"So what do I do? Just let my baby lose all his amniotic fluid and what, sit around and do nothing?"

"Isn't there something more your doctor can do, run some tests, something?"

"Like I know?"

The doctor returns and I click off with Rick. I listen as he lays out a schedule of ultrasounds. One early next week just to be sure. When I open my mouth, he cuts me off explaining that it's probably nothing. "My suggestion, get some rest."

In the parking lot, I am about to climb gingerly into my convertible. It's nearly five on a bright April afternoon and I feel some confidence come creeping back. The pain in my stomach, the baby losing a little amniotic fluid; it's probably nothing. I can hear the doctor's words echoing in my head and they do sound oddly reassuring. Then a hurt shoots through my body bending me in half and throwing me to the ground so fast I don't have time to put out an arm. I hit the pavement with my hip and shoulder and roll onto my back. I don't feel a thing from the impact because the ache in my belly is so intense. Stab wound intense. It consumes me. For a moment I can't see or hear or think. Then I begin to shiver involuntarily and a stunning, pulsing throb washes over me, as if I was dipped in the icy waters of the Atlantic fully clothed. I'm freezing, my teeth are banging against each other in loud clanking sounds, and my legs and shoulders go all goose-pimply.

The pavement is sucking the warmth right out of me.

A security guard sees me lying there next to my car and strides over, stopping a good ten paces away. If he carried a gun, which he doesn't, he'd be in one of those hand-on-gun positions they teach at guard school.

"Ma'am," he says.

"I'm pregnant," I say.

"Ma'am?"

"Something's wrong. Can you get some help?"

He radios the emergency room the problem and then reaches down and helps me to sit up. Eventually I stand. I put my arm around him and we shuffle to the ER entrance on the other side of the building. On our little stroll through the parking lot, I untangle myself from the guard, a good and decent man with strong arms, call Rick and tell him I've collapsed. "Come. Now."

"Get to the ER as fast as you can," he says.

"Please, I need you here with me."

I hear him muffled in the background, barking orders to a nurse. To me he says, "You need to get to emergency."

An hour-plus later Rick arrives at the hospital. By then, the ER doctor has run me through a great bugaboo of tests and calibrations and moon phases and come up with absolutely nada, like my trifling collapse in the parking lot was all a shameless plea for attention. What I want is to know what's happening on the inside, down around my uterus where it feels as though my boys are having a rousing game of kickball.

The nurses put me in an alcove of my own where Rick and I stare at each other. He holds my hand to keep the blood in my fingers from freezing solid, and we do a lot of frowning because we've got squat to do until the results of the tests come back. Eventually the ER doc, Dr. Elliott, a rough, slight kid who looks like a Wyoming cowboy or a professional Frisbee player or both, returns with my chart, holding the plastic clipboard loosely in one hand as if he might give it a good fling at any moment. "I'm sorry." He says. "Nothing conclusive. It's probably a urinary tract infection."

"I see," Rick says in that nice way of his that means he's not buying it. "What about chorioamnionitis?"

"What?" I say, though I'm not sure I want to hear.

Dr. Elliot glances at Rick as if deciding who goes first. When Rick doesn't answer, the doctor says, "It's an inflammation of the fetal membranes due to infection." Then to Rick as if I'm not sitting right there, says, "She'd be tender in the belly. That's not the case."

"That is the case," I say. "I lost it in the parking lot. I'm tender, trust me." At that moment, I let loose a quaking shiver, a solid three point five on the Richter. Both men stare at me. "It's cold in here," I say.

Dr. Frisbee casually reaches over and pokes me in the belly. "Does that hurt?"

"No."

"Here?"

"No.

"Here?"

"Well."

"I'm no specialist, but if you had chorioamnionitis, you'd be hyper-sensitive to touch."

"What about other symptoms?" I say.

"It's not chorioamnionitis," he says confidently, then changes his mind. "I'm pretty sure it's not."

"Here, take this." He hands me a prescription for antibiotics. "Go home. Get some rest. See your OB/GYN in the morning. I'm afraid that's the best I can offer at the moment. Don't worry. I'm sure it's nothing."

Why is it all the men in my life keep telling me not to worry when all I want to do is worry and, if you ask me, I have a solid foundation of worry-generating activities staring me in the face.

I don't want to drive home, afraid I might have another attention-grabbing collapse while behind the wheel. We crawl into Rick's car and he drives while I moan. We can pick up my car tomorrow, he tells me, though I couldn't care less. I've got bigger problems and bigger worries and bigger everything on my mind. I've got pains that mean something and I don't know what that something is and no one is telling or they don't know and either way, the meaning of the hurt matters to me. Rick glances at me from time to time, taking in the sparest nuance of gesture. We don't talk. We worry. We think and scheme and assess and I, for one, pray for a benevolent intervention. *Please Lord, make it be nothing. Make whatever's wrong with me easily fixable or insignificant. Or make it laughable, the way chest pains can turn out to be a determined but benign case of flatulence. Make it painful even if that's your wish, but make it safe for my babies.* We cruise across the Bay Bridge and back home. We sit in the living room. "Honey," Rick says to me, sitting there on the couch. "You don't look too good."

"I'm not sure what's happening."

"You look flushed. Are you hot?"

"Cold."

"Dizzy, fatigued?"

"What?"

Rick tilts his head to one side and watches me.

He puts me to bed, gives me two large white pills to swallow, antibiotics, and just as the pills hit my stomach another shock of pain overtakes me. I try to fall asleep but I can't, I'm in and out of a state of throbbing soreness, but soreness is not near the right word. I need a new word, a cross between exhaustion and chills and flashes of heat that burn from the inside out. I want to douse myself in water or some new chemical fire retardant that promises to squelch the fire in an instant, a new fangled compound that slithers into the pores of your skin and robs the fire of its oxygen. Then, inexplicably, I'm cold again, freezing, and I wrap myself in blankets that only keep the cold in and I half-seriously consider crawling into our oversized oven or just cranking the knob to high and squatting there on the tile floor in front of the open door. I go from one fit of chills and teeth chattering shakes to another. I'm so weak I can't speak, so I just lie on my side and shiver.

Rick checks in on me. "What the hell?" He presses on my forehead with the back of his hand. "For chrissakes. We're going to the hospital!"

"What?"

"I've got to get you to the ER."

"Are you sure?"

"Absolutely."

I think about it for a brief second. "Okay," I say. "Okay."

By now it's the wee hours of the morning and on the way, he calls my OB/GYN, Dr. Gomez, and tells her something is terribly wrong. The pregnancy has gotten fouled up and his lovely wife, me, has severe, persistent abdominal pain. This last part, the severe, persistent pain part, he says slowly, letting each word sink in before moving on to the next like you might while talking to someone only half listening. He pauses, the phone pressed hard to his ear with one hand, the other hand on the steering wheel navigating turns. The doctor says she'll arrange to have me admitted and hangs up. Or, I think that's what she says.

We arrive at the hospital where Rick has worked for the last twenty years. Up we go to obstetrics on the second floor, me shuffling along not fully aware what's going on or where we are exactly. A soft-handed nurse ushers me into an exam room and asks me to undress and don one of those shamefully skimpy hospital gowns. I mostly just stand there and hold the gown until Rick comes in and helps me unbutton and unzip and undo whatever needs to be undone and slips the gown over my neck and ties it in back. Normally this wouldn't be a chore, but my brain has shut down and the sting in my tummy makes any movement agonizing. For a moment, I feel giddy and my very own gynecologist, Dr. Gomez, shows up, her mouth a thin smile but her eyes giving herself away. The concern radiating from her eyes shoots out in all directions. She orders me up on the table where I spread my legs without being told and she gives my pelvis and all parts nearby a good going over.

Dr. Gomez stands, pulls off her gloves and drops them into a clinical-looking wastebasket. "I'll be right back," she says.

"What can you tell us?" Rick says.

"I'd like to consult with Dr. Romero before saying more," she says.

Moments later, she returns. She peers strangely at me, or is it a grimace, and says to Rick, "We have a major infection in the uterus."

"And," Rick says.

"There is no easy way to say this."

I glance at my husband, his face a stone hard mask, a face used to steadying itself for bad news.

Don't say it, I tell the universe. *Not out loud. Don't say the words. Don't say it.*

Chapter Nine

Losing the Twins

"You're going to lose the babies," Dr. Gomez says.

"No," I say. "Rick, honey, please don't let them take the babies." I reach for Rick's hand, the smooth fingers moving slightly, involuntarily, tapping against the faded blue of his jeans, but I think better of it knowing that some new hurt will bite me if I move even an inch.

The doctor glances down at me. I know what she's thinking, but she's wrong. She's thinking I'm one of those unreasonable patients, say your typical car accident victim or slip-and-faller who has gotten herself a nice bonk on the head and now makes not one bit of sense. That's not me, I want to tell her, but the ache in my tummy rockets down into my butt and legs and all I manage is an eye-squeezing wince that lasts so long the muscles in my cheeks begin to cramp. She says, "It's likely that a leak in amniotic fluid infected your uterus. The infection spread to one baby. And then the other. I'm sorry, there's nothing we can do."

Twelve hours ago I was an expectant mother. Now, I have no babies. Just like that.

My voice is screechy and hoarse at the same time because I'm on the verge of hysteria. How many other women lay here on this very table listening to the news: It's over. The last five months of dreaming, forget about it. Move on. She doesn't say it, but I half expect her to. "You can always try again." I make some effort to turn my head but a new tingle of hurt shoots up my spine and I twist my face fully into the pillow hoping the pain is somehow connected to my voice and will politely go away if I stop talking. Only I can't stop talking. "Can't you just take the infected one?" I say to my pillow.

"What?" the doctor says.

"It's okay," Rick says. "Everything's going to be okay."

I repeat myself, but even I don't understand a word of it.

"Can we lose one of the babies," Rick says reading my mind. My husband is as solid as an Icelandic ice cap, but I sense he's beginning to melt. I hear something in his voice I've never heard, nothing a stranger would pick up, but a lowness in his timbre that spells trouble.

The doctor, a slight woman with faded freckles on her nose and cheeks I'd never noticed before, gives me a look, one of those elbows-to-the-table arm wrestling sorts of looks that says she'd rather not argue this one out but will if she has to. To me, she says, "The lower one, you mean?"

"Yes, yes," Rick says for me. "And save the other?"

"No," she says flatly as if there's no getting through to Rick or me.

"Why?" I ask.

"Both babies are dead. I'm sorry."

"Or badly infected," Rick says now switching teams, siding with Dr. Gomez. His voice is so soft it's barely perceptible in the hushed chatter and muffled mechanical sounds of obstetrics.

"Or so badly infected," the doctor says, thankful for a little help, "they won't survive."

I twist onto my side and back and thankfully no new phantom pain pokes or stabs at me. "Can you at least try?" I ask, staring at the ceiling.

"It's over," she says, and I can tell she's reticent to say it, to pronounce the words so simply, so plainly, with such finality. "My job now is to take care of you."

I roll on my side and tears begin a slow trickle from the corner of my eye down my cheek and into my ear. So this is what a waking nightmare feels like. When we entered the hospital, I believed we had a chance. I secretly believed we could make it. I'd spent the previous week buying baby clothes and I picked up a pair of the cutest retro olive green onesie's with a cartoon of a baby Popeye on the front and the words "Strong to the Finish" above Popeye holding a sippy cup presumably filled with drinkable spinach. I bought furniture, an antique looking hardwood cradle, and I finally selected a paint color, a light shade of aqua, for the babies' room. Now, none of that matters. Tears run down my face and into my ear and when the small depression in my ear fill, I hear tears hit the protective paper covering the exam table. I want to roll over, away from Dr. Gomez and Rick and everyone I know or ever will know and disappear. I want to vanish. Poof. Gone. And I want to take my grief, if that's what it is, with me and protect it and nurture it so that I never forget my two baby boys, now drowning in infection and hurting like I hurt. Exactly like I hurt. It just occurs to me that I might not be feeling my pain at all but my baby's pain. This ache in my belly and back and legs and places I can't even identify, is, I'm convinced, their pain. My baby boys are communicating with me the only way they can, by kicking and scratching at my insides with all their might. They want out. I somehow believe the hurt means they are alive. Only when the hurt stops are my babies beyond hope.

"What's next?" Rick asks the doctor.

"We terminate the pregnancy."

"Isn't that redundant," Rick says. He's being argumentative, unlike him in all ways and I get that he's hurting, too.

"We'll give your wife a vaginal suppository." The doctor puts a hand on my shoulder. "The medication will cause you to go into labor and expel the two fetuses."

I see that we went from babies to fetuses in the last two seconds.

"My babies aren't dead," I say.

"Dead," she says. "Or horribly infected. I'm sorry this is so difficult, but yes, they're dead."

"Not yet," I say. "I'm sure of it."

"Let's get this over with," Rick says.

The staff gets me admitted and moved to a private room. The room has one bed and a recliner that Rick collapses into, exhausted. He inhales a giant breath and releases an unquestionably defeated exhale. Shortly after I settle in, a priest arrives and talks to me about losing the babies. They're not dead, I tell him, and he pauses for a moment and glances up at Rick and back to me and begins again. I only hear the hum of his gravelly voice, not the words. His pensiveness infects the room. I get the suppository and Rick and I wait for the labor pains to begin. They do. I'm fully in labor, or at least I get the thrill of gut-wrenching stomach-groin-back pain that comes at me in angry waves. Only the babies don't come. We wait and wait. And wait. In late afternoon, a nurse pokes her head into the room. "Nothing's happening," I say.

"Sometimes it doesn't work." She looks worried and scared.

"It's not your fault," I say.

"Oh," the nurse says, frowns, and turns away.

Rick is standing, hands in his pockets, neck craned up at the TV high on the wall. He cocks his head to listen but doesn't face me.

"I'll talk to the doctor," the nurse says not so much to me but to the room. "She'll likely recommend a shot."

Meanwhile, I'm wilting, growing sicker and weaker with each passing minute. I have an infection all up inside me, my entire body aches, and I can't think straight. I sleep and wake. It's dark outside my window with evening or night or whatever. Nothing's happening and the babies are still inside of me. Rick is half lying, half sitting, in the recliner beside my bed. I say, "Is this right?"

"Right?"

"This isn't right."

"There's nothing right about it," he says, and I smile back at him but don't truly understand what we're talking about. His voice is mournful, patient. "According to Gomez, the shots can take a while."

"I don't want to lose the babies," I say.

"I know."

"They're alive, I think"

"I know."

We've joined the small club of grieving parents who don't want to think about the present, this frozen moment in time. It's the posture of people wanting to put off current pain, willing to experience any amount of suffering, but at a later date when there's more time, space, and perspective. Rick and I are people addicted to the positive and the possible, already perhaps subconsciously understanding that this unstoppable chain of events may eventually lead to something better, less cruel, and more meaningful.

I'm spent mentally and emotionally. Physically. The nurse has pumped me full of pain meds, fluids and antibiotics and I feel as if I could pop. Popping would be an improvement, a tiny step forward and an inch closer to what's next. Rick is only half in this world. He's not really paying attention, not reasoning through the possible complications like his typical cardiologist self. He has put his trust in Dr. Gomez, a nice woman who takes her time and consults her husband, Dr. Romero, the superstar GYN/Urology specialist. We haven't seen the good doctors in hours, but the nurses have, and they occasionally drop in to tell us what's on the doctors' minds. I don't know if I say it out loud or only think it. Dr. Gomez knows what she's talking about, right? She knows about labor inducing suppositories and fetus aborting meds and septic shock. She knows about infected babies. Right? I mean we're not just taking her word this is the right approach. Right? I don't recall if I ever get an answer. All I know is that nothing's working as it should. I don't go into labor, not the kind of labor where you produce a baby. I don't promptly expel the twins. Instead, I grow sicker. Then Rick gets this unfamiliar look on his face. It's the look of worry. Then I start to worry.

I'm getting worse.

Hours pass. Then the hours turn to a day.

I can't hold a thought for more than, well, I can't hold a thought for any length of time. I hear the nurse tell Rick that my urine output has dropped. Great. On top of everything else, I can't pee. Rick demands to see the doctor who, in my confused state, magically appears. He, Rick, asks for a "pulse ox," a measure of the oxygen in my blood and the nurse snaps a little black plastic device over the end of my index finger and stares at the digital readout. The nurse frowns at the readout, then at the doctor and steps out of the way. A tentative Dr. Gomez steps up to my bed and out of reflex reaches into her pocket for a pen, poised to write something down. Another doctor appears, called in by Dr. Gomez. He is a tall man with a head so far away it looks hazy and blurred. He lifts my hand and looks at the readout on the pulse ox doohickey. "Low," he says in a booming voice. "In the 70 percent range. This should be 98, 99." He comes off as angry, as if someone is to blame for my low oxygen output. To Rick, he says, "I think we have a blood clot to the lung. I can't be sure, but I'm thinking pulmonary embolism. We need a CTA."

"That's ridiculous," Rick says.

"I understand your concern," Dr. Gomez says.

"It's far more likely she's experiencing noncardiogenic pulmonary edema. She's septic. Her lungs are filling with fluid. Her organs are shutting down, and if I'm right, the CTA will only make things worse. You inject dye into someone whose kidneys are shutting down, and you could put her into complete renal failure."

"It's important," Dr. Gomez says, "that we look at this calmly."

"What about adult respiratory distress?" Rick says.

"I don't know. Could be," the blurry doctor says.

"A contrast injection could worsen the leakage and damage her lungs and kidneys," Rick says.

"I suggest we wait," Dr. Gomez says, "If we give it a little more time—"

"My wife's organs are shutting down."

"What do you suggest?" the blurry doctor says.

"I want Dr. Karras to see her right away. And we need to move her to the OR for a Cesarean section. Now."

"Sounds reasonable," the voice says.

"I'm not sure the c-section is prudent at this juncture," Dr. Gomez says.

"These babies have to come out now. We can't stand around waiting for the medications to run their course."

"Let's calm down," Dr. Gomez says.

"The medications aren't working."

"Shouting at me doesn't help."

"Her kidneys are shutting down. Just how long do you propose we wait?"

"You may be overstating your case."

"And if I'm not?"

Dr. Gomez gives a nervous look up to the other doctor, as if she's no longer sure whose side he's on. She does something with her lips, mouthing words I can't hear or rehearsing what she's about to say, just stalling, and the muscles in her jaw delicately moving side to side. She does not look at him, but speaks to my husband. "Dr. Simons, I'm doing the best I can. I assure you."

"Do something or she's going to die."

"The CTA might be our best option," she says.

"This is wrong," Rick says. "We're not doing the scan."

Dr. Gomez shies away from my bed like a scolded child, turns, and softly pads out of the room. Rick yanks out his cell and dials Dr. Karras, or Dr. K as he is known within the hospital, who specializes in critical care medicine. Within minutes Dr. K arrives.

"K," Rick says, "we need to talk to the surgeon, the anesthesiologist, she needs to be in the OR. Can you help make this happen?"

Dr. K is a small man, slender with hunched shoulders, in his late thirties. He is all business and speaks rapidly in mangled English with a Middle Eastern accent.

I can't breathe. I'm confused, panicky.

Dr. K stares at me, his face giving nothing away. "Toxic metabolic encephalopathy."

"I agree," Rick says.

"I want a chest x-ray and arterial blood gas," Dr. K says to the nurse. Time passes quickly and the results of the tests show pulmonary edema, low blood oxygen, and adult respiratory distress syndrome just as Rick suspected. K says, "Considering one or both of the fetuses are infected, I recommend immediate c-section."

Rick pulls out his cell and jabs at the numbers. Dr. Gomez answers and Rick demands she perform a c-section.

Dr. Gomez arrives with her husband, Dr. Romero, who stares at me and shakes his head. He doesn't review my chart, doesn't ask how I feel, doesn't do anything but look at me for a long moment. "Get her to the OR."

I'm dog sick and go in and out of consciousness as the nurses wheel me to the operating room. One or both of the nurses talk in low whispers giving me a preview of what's to come. I only half listen. I perk up when I hear I'll have a breathing tube down my throat when I wake. Oh boy. Then I'm out again.

As surgeries go, this one is ugly. Once the doctor opens me up she finds a uterus full of pus along with two dead babies. She scoops out the babies and hoses out my insides and sews me up. The entire operation takes twenty minutes. I'm wheeled off to a room in the intensive care unit. My new abode has a bed and a glass wall looking into the nurses' station. During surgery I get intubated, as promised, a fancy word for shoving a tube down your throat and pumping air in and out of your lungs, and the tube stays in place after the surgery. It doesn't bother me, because I'm out cold for two solid days. Rick takes his post lying on an uncomfortable cot—no recliner available—next to the bed.

Even after the surgery, Rick is worried my good doctors will screw something up. He is angry they let my infection go on as long as they did before surgically removing the source of the infection, my own dead babies. He's afraid he might lose his blushing bride before we really get startedand thus refuses to leave my bedside for anything but the occasional sprint to the bathroom or down the hall for a sandwich from the vending machine. He spends a good portion of his time looking at my chart, checking my vitals, examining my breathing tube and intravenous lines for hairline cracks and invisible signs of structural failure. With a smidgen more room in my bed, I've no doubt he would have crawled in and wrapped himself around me, cocoon-like, to keep me safe. He stays close enough to protect me from external forces like careless nurses and incompetent doctors, a position that has softened with time, but in those hours after surgery any doctor who approaches is considered bungling and incompetent until proven otherwise. Were it possible, he would have opened me up and crawled inside and stood guard, daring even the smallest poisonous cell to get past him. The surgery has staved off death, but Rick isn't celebrating any time soon. He worries and fidgets and pries at the edges of my treatment. He is close but not close enough to protect me from my own body and one of several intimidating infections still trying their damnedist to kill me.

On the morning of day two, my eyes open and a nurse yanks the tube out of my throat. I take my first raspy, unassisted gasp for air since losing the twins. I glance around, get my bearings, and remember why I'm here. I begin to cry. Rick stares at me, his doctor's analytical mind working away trying to devise a way to make it all better, a man who wants nothing out of life so much as to ease a patient's pain, and here he has a wife and patient, though not his patient exactly, sobbing these big, wet, sloppy tears right in front of him and there's not a thing he can do to make the pain, guilt, and loss one iota less heartbreaking. But there is nothing I want him or anyone to say or do. On the contrary, I want to feel the loss, to sink down and have the warmth of defeat wrap itself around me and squeeze me until my insides nearly burst. I want to suffer this twinge of misery, to take it in with my entire body and imprint this achy awareness of what might have been somewhere in the recess of my brain. Years or decades from now, when I can no longer remember what it was like to carry two small babies and feel them growing inside me for five long months, I want to remember the hurt and the muscle ache and the infection doing its best to take my life and almost succeeding. Thinking these thoughts, a flash of relief washes over me. The kind of relief you get from putting a bad event firmly behind you, as if that's even possible. I'm alive, I tell myself. Then the relief vanishes as quickly as it arrived. A trouncing loss fills my head and body, and cry and cry and don't bother to wipe away the tears.

A nurse watches me. She doesn't move to help or make me stop or hurry me in any way. No subtle, "Let's get on with it" cues in her body language. She is a woman accustomed to medical hammerings and the accompanying unhappiness. She knows, or so I imagine, that all the crying is just one more step in the process of being human, of the magic of turning eggs and sperm into babies, and losing those babies this close to the finish line. And getting on with life.

"She's out of the woods," the nurse says. I can't tell if it's a question or a statement. She says, "You've had two beautiful baby boys. They will be with you forever."

"What we had," Rick says in a toneless voice, "was a nightmare."

He doesn't take his eyes off of me.

Tears well up and puddle on his lower lid. "I was that close," he says, and he means that close to losing me.

I part my lips and for the first time feel my damaged throat. I swallow hard and imagine the words and I imagine he understands my thoughts. It doesn't matter. I know what he feels. My husband is a thinker, a considerer of moves and counter moves, and seldom initiates any action without first allowing for all the possible ramifications. "We lost the twins" has consequences and he stands over me, his hair partially in his face, considering what those consequences will be without saying a thing. He doesn't have to.

I try to speak but nothing comes out. My throat is swollen and I have to force the air out of my mouth to make a sound. I take a deep breath and push the air up and out my throat. "I love you," I whisper.

"Don't talk."

Rick leans over to kiss me and when his face is inches from mine, I say, "It's my fault."

"Don't talk."

"The boys were my responsibility."

"Ours," he says. "Don't talk."

"I messed up. Now they're dead."

"We messed up."

"It's over."

"We'll try again."

"After all this?"

"After all this," he says.

The sobbing and breathing take their toll and I don't have the strength to tell my husband I do, I will, after all this I'm willing to risk it all again if that's what it takes to make a baby.

The nurse asks if Rick wants to see the boys. I'm out cold, way deep under some powerful drug the nurse had slipped into the stream of my IV, but Rick tells me what happens. The nurse stares at him waiting for an answer. She's stumped him. He doesn't know what to say and stalls, running the calculations of action and consequence: view the babies and be overjoyed (unlikely), repulsed (more likely), or possibly fall off the edge of the world into a deep depression, the image of our two dead twins haunting him for years (likelihood unknown).

"I guess so," he says.

The nurse leaves the room and returns carrying a tiny bassinet, she calls it, but it's not. It's nothing more than a sturdy box with a lid that comes off and inside the box is a blue blanket with its flaps covering two small lumps. She holds the box as Rick gently pulls back the blanket, a sort of fine fleece, and he stares down at two very small, slightly shriveled babies. At nineteen weeks, the babies are as light as feathers and about the length of his hand. The faces are surprisingly human, the expressions indifferent, almost peaceful. Rick watches, secretly wishing for movement, some sign of life, a twitch or wriggle or a wink, but that doesn't happen and he realizes only in hindsight that he's made a very big mistake. He never should have looked, never should have agreed to this self-imposed torture. What he should have said was, "No thank you. Not me. Not on your life, ma'am."

What he does say is, "Do not offer to show these to my wife." He folds the blue fleece delicately on top of the boys, and can't stop himself from tucking the blanket in around them, pressing the folds between one tiny body and the cold cardboard of the box.

"It's a choice we give all parents," the nurse says. "It's just—"

"Do you understand me?" He says this in a calm, commanding voice, meant to express that she knows mighty damn little about what's best for this patient, me, and protocol or no protocol he's made his decision. He knows how he sounds, like an angry father, a pompous doctor, or just a man not fully in charge of his emotions who chooses to exert himself by bullying the first person he sees. My husband is none of these, of course. He's a man who loves me and doesn't want to see me suffer if it can be avoided. At the same time, he looks at the nurse, a woman he has known and seen around the hospital for many years, a very good nurse in his estimation, a person with a real capacity for compassion. He places the lid of the bassinet—a word he likes after all—on top of the box and jimmies it slowly in place. Even with the lid in place he pictures the boys laying there side-by-side, spooning, keeping each other company like good brothers do, and it's a picture that never goes away, is forever in the back of his mind even when he wishes it wasn't. Long after we leave the hospital, and for years to come, he occasionally recalls the sight of the boys in the bassinette and cries. Mostly when I'm not around, he takes a private moment to remember, reflect, and consider what might have been but wasn't.

At nineteen weeks the boys are only three weeks short of being viable, Rick's words not mine. At twenty-two weeks, had the doctors whisked them from a healthy womb, their chance of survival in a neonatal intensive care until would have been reasonable. Twenty-two weeks is that magical milestone where modern science can take over. At nineteen weeks, there just isn't enough magic to keep a baby alive; two babies, impossible. The way it went down, it's likely we would have lost them anyway. Rick refers to the debacle as a geographic tragedy—the lower twin implanted too low in the uterus. As the lower twin grew, the amniotic sac got closer and closer to the cervix and thus more vulnerable to causing an infection. The lower twin's bad luck doomed his brother.

A day later, I turn some kind of corner. The nurse lets me get out of bed, shuffle across the room, and go to the toilet by myself. After that first pee, I recover quickly. The antibiotics kick in and the infection disappears. Rick says it's my strong Swedish stock. Dr. K shows up and looks me over and won't stop talking about how quickly I returned to health. He and Rick swap stories of the longest and shortest recoveries, both of them pretty sure I hold the record for the shortest. They gab about how all they get is old geezers who take forever to heal, if they ever do, how they'd almost forgotten what it was like to work with anyone under the mid-century mark. Most of their patients, Dr. K tells me, or at least those in the sexagenarian range and on up, would positively take three or more weeks to recover from an ordeal like mine. With me, it's three days. It's hard to tell if all this is a show or the real thing, if they're trying to lift my spirits or are genuinely shocked at how resilient the human body can be when it wants to. I'd come through renal failure, a shocked lung, sepsis, blood transfusions, and had that lousy tube crammed down my throat and three days later, here I am almost ready to skedaddle. Oh, and don't forget that gruesome c-section, the incision still tender.

I spend another day in the hospital on my back watching daytime TV. Tom Cruise and Katie Holmes are due to have their baby any day. Baby watch is what they're calling it. Every time they mention it, I start to cry. Rick and I, we don't name our baby boys. What's the point? On the day of my discharge, a nurse hands me an official-looking document. I'm reluctant to call it a birth certificate. On it Twin A is listed as nine ounces and Twin B eight ounces. At the bottom of the page are tiny footprints for each boy. Delivery date: Saturday, April 8, at 10:43 p.m. and 10:44 p.m. the cert says. I also receive a photo of the babies. The photo is wrapped in a blue fleece blanket inside a little cardboard box. Rick looks at the photo and scolds me to not to look. Not even a peek. "You won't like it," he says. "I mean it. No good can come from it."

I'm good at taking advice. I never look at the pictures. I don't throw the box away, but I don't look.

Rick gets me discharged from the ICU to home, an uncommon occurrence, and off we go, wheeled out of the hospital right to Rick's car. We drive home to our big empty house. My grandmother used to say, "What doesn't kill you makes you stronger." After we get home, I lay in bed and think, well, it didn't kill me. So, I must be stronger. Only I don't get stronger. I get worse. Blisters develop around and inside of my mouth, which make eating and drinking about as pleasant as having your fingernails yanked. I don't put a thing down my gullet for ten straight days. Finally the blisters vanish. I take it easy and let my body catch up with the rest of me. At some point, I recall sitting with Rick out back on the deck watching the tugboats amble up the Nanticoke. I look over and say, "What just happened?"

He doesn't ask what I mean, but simply shakes his head as if to say, "I wish I could tell you."

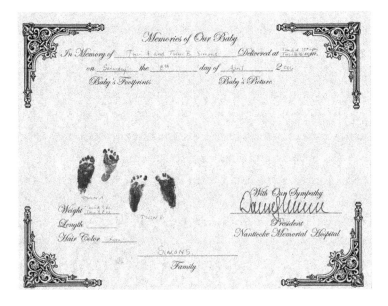

Chapter Ten

Good Counsel

·······································

I had gone directly home to recuperate. Didn't pass Go. Didn't collect 200 dollars. I get a few visitors at home, but I'm lousy company and I want to be alone. Rick suggests that I talk to someone, code words for, "Why don't you hook up with a shrink?" He doesn't say it directly because my husband is kind and when feelings are at stake, he prefers to let things take their own sweet time. If the problem was as simple as a faulty heart valve, a pulsing vessel, or a bottleneck in the blood flow department, he'd be as straightforward as Judge Wapner. Only my problem isn't any of those. My problem is harder to get your arms around. I'd lost my babies and secretly, though I didn't tell a soul, I blame myself.

My best friends, Renee, Lisa, and Tonya have all come running in some form or fashion. While I was in the hospital, Renee was stuck way up in Manhasset, New York, and couldn't get away but called every couple of hours trying her best to be there for me. My little near-death experience took place while Lisa sat on a bleacher in Baltimore watching her daughter pom-pom her heart out at a cheer competition. As soon as she heard the news she ditched the competition, climbed in her car and hauled ass down I-97 turning a three-hour slog through traffic into a two-hour sprint. She arrived at the hospital half loony with worry and exhaustion, but did her best to be comforting and supportive. Tonya lives less than an hour away and was by my side for much of the fireworks.

Back at home, all three want to mother me and I'm having none of it. Then my parents arrive and my flesh and blood mother begins mothering me in a way only a real mother can. It's all too much. I have my very own support group, a pride of people who love me and want only the best for me, people sending out good vibes to God above and all I can think is that I've done something wrong. So wrong I had to lose my babies as payback.

I lie in bed and mull over what I could have done differently, what I could have done or not done to prevent that first domino from falling.

Friends send cards, flowers, meatloaves, and other things less sensible. Rick gently props the cards on the dresser so I can see them from my bed. The bright vases and billowing flowers he places around the bedroom like a less than confident interior designer who wants nothing more than to please his client, me.

"Like this," he says twisting a bouquet of long stemmed red and yellow roses so that the reds mostly point at the bed.

"It's fine," I say and then stare at the bathroom door, at the trim around the door and the joint at the top where the wood has warped, shrunk, or whatever wood does when it gets old and tired.

"Or this." Rick moves the vase four inches to the left into the sunlight. He is trying to engage me. It's a trick, something he'd read in a book that will help my brooding mind move from opportunities lost onto to cheerier topics.

The roses look good. Delightful. Bouncy. Happy. As do the lisianthus, daisy poms and waxflower in the corner. And the mound of stargazer lilies against the far wall. "Perfect." I say it with a tablespoon of sarcasm, just enough to keep him guessing.

He moves to the dresser and lifts a card from a bouquet of roses, daisies and snapdragons, all of them white as baby powder. "The card says it's a sympathy arrangement." He frowns at the card.

"I'm tired."

"No really, where would you like these?" he says.

"Leave it where it is. It's fine, really."

Rick glances at the card, at the flowers, and at me. He reaches for a rose and rubs the petal between his thumb and finger. Maybe he's tempted to lean over and put his nose right in there where things are lush and breathe in until his chest hurts, but he doesn't. He shakes his head as if something's going on and whatever it is it's just out of reach. I know how my husband thinks and what he's thinking is why is such a beautiful arrangement of white flowers referred to as a sympathy bouquet. Is it the whiteness? Is it the individual flowers or the smells or some other cosmic connection only a committed botanist would understand? Do white snapdragons, white carnations, and colossal white football mums exude more sympathy than say a single red rose? Mostly, what he's wondering is why with all the color and flowery tang leaking into the room and the extravagant arrangements oozing sympathy am I still in such a funk?

At some point everybody scrams from the house. Rick drives my parents to the airport and they fly home. Tonya cuts back on the daily visits, Lisa stops trekking from New Jersey, and Renee cuts back to Monday-Wednesday-Friday calls from Long Island. Then it's all me, stuck in this big house on the river. Me and the rowdy barges outside my window chugging up and down the Nanticoke. I'm well enough to get out of bed. But why bother? I sit and stare out the window at two giant white ash trees, their branches going every which way and the newly budding baby leaves fluttering without a care in the world. I can't see the river from the bed. When no one's around, I get up, stand next to the window and look out at the wide flat lawn, the river, and the forest on the other side of the river. Or I sit up and glare at the walls, the hardwood floors, and the crown molding and wonder what's wrong with me. I live in a house descended from heaven and I don't even like it. Some days, I think I hate it.

My hesitant OB/GYN doctor left me with an ever-present reminder of the ordeal—a lovely purple scar across my belly, which itches, and I find myself absently rubbing a finger across the length of the bumpy thing until I catch myself and stop. I'm tired, my body aches and I stay in bed for a week watching the news and daytime TV. I'm bombarded with Tom Cruise's big-toothed face and his newborn, little Suri in his arms, the kid already trying to show some gums for the camera. You'd have to be from Venus not to get the idea that Suri's birth is miraculous and newsworthy.

For a week I see and hear nothing but baby noises. Laughter and little baby cries come at me from all angles.

Rick says, "Have you given any thought to seeing someone?"

"You think I need it?" I ask. I'm listless and occasionally shuffle from the bedroom to the kitchen often forgetting what it was I wanted. I don't answer the phone. I've stopped wearing makeup. I shower, but only out of habit; with a modicum of willpower, I might stop that as well. I don't talk so much as mumble. Sometimes I just hum the words and wait and see how much my husband understands or intuits. Sometimes he guesses all wrong, and I say, "That's it. Whatever you said. Do that."

Rick sits on the end of the bed facing away from me, his shoulders pointing at the TV and his head facing the door. "It can't hurt."

"What if it does?"

"Does what?"

"Hurt."

"I know a woman," he says. "Not personally, but I know of her. She's good, from what I hear."

"She's good," I say and let that hang there.

"I think you should see a counselor. It's up to you, but I think it's a good idea."

So I see a counselor.

In the middle of May the weather mercifully nudges into the sixties after a couple of months of frigid thirties and forties. By now I'm strong enough to venture out of the house and meet with Pam, my counselor. She's a woman with rounded features and soft skin who looks right at home cozying up to people in the later stages of terminal illness, or those addicted to family dramas, or people like me who just want to make some sense of losing twin boys.

Put your emotions on the back burner, all the baby loss literature says, and it'll bite you in the ass later. I don't want any late-stage ass biting, so I do what I know I should, which is get out of the house and go spill my guts to a stranger. Pam has an office in Maryland about forty-five minutes away. When I spot the address, I give the fading house numbers a long hard stare to make sure I'm in the right place. The building is in fact an old home that looks like it was built sometime in the twenties. I'm not sure of the color—whitish, discolored gray, or maybe even avocado. I pull around to the back and the rear of the house is dowdier than the front.

Up to now, I'd never been to a shrink of any flavor. I'm the sort who suffers setbacks and then just as quickly picks up the pieces and keeps moving. Movement is my cure-all. Whatever happens, keep moving is my advice, only I haven't kept moving. I'm stuck in neutral, sitting here in my car wondering why I can't get my life into drive.

I park, climb a wooden staircase, open the door, and walk into a wide hallway with sloping wooden floors, just as Pam's cheery voice instructed me to do. I do all this briskly and with purpose before I change my mind. The back entrance is for crazies like me who can enter without being seen from the street. In hindsight it sounds silly, but I'm embarrassed to be here, embarrassed that I need help of any sort, downright humiliated that the help I apparently need is in the I-just-want-to-make-sure-I'm-not-a-nutcase department.

Inside, it's as quaint as any grandmother's home that hasn't had a good scrubbing in the last decade. I see the sign for Pam's office along with neatly hand-painted signs for two other businesses—a massage therapist squeezed into what might have once been the living room and an antique store where the kitchen-dining room once was.

Pam had given me clear instructions. "Be early," she said on the phone. "Come on in and take a seat on the couch outside my office. You can't miss it. Make yourself comfortable. When it's time, I'll come get you."

True enough. I don't miss the couch. It looks like something a college kid might drag in from the sidewalk. I think twice before plopping down on it, then I resign myself to the entire experience and sit. At three sharp I hear the floor in the office creak. Pam opens her door, introduces herself and in we go.

Pam has a metal desk and chair combo against the wall with a window and a couple of sidewalk chairs that more or less match the couch. The chairs are politely angled toward each other and she motions with her chin for me to choose a chair. I do and she rests her soft round body into the other.

Pam is in her forties, with long hair, soft voice – all the trappings of a good counselor. She wears plain slacks, a plain sweater, and a single plain faux-silver bracelet on her wrist. Here I am, ready to pour out my soul to a stranger trained in listening without yawning. I wait for some insightful question, some probing remark that makes me think seriously about my own mortality and my place in the world, some clever aside that offers a new and hopeful perspective on relationships, pregnancy, and dead babies.

Pam says, "May I see your insurance card?"

I hand over the card and she gets up, leaves the room and runs a copy using a hundred-year-old copier out in the hall that makes sad whining noises. From the hall, she says, "I see here there's a twenty dollar co-pay."

I can tell she's embarrassed to ask. I reach into my purse for two tens.

She takes the tens and quickly shoves them into her pocket. She hands me my insurance card and takes her seat, ready for blast off. "Okay," she says and waits for me to say something. I don't. She says, "Why are you here?"

Her directness startles me.

Honestly, I don't know what to say. *I'm here because...* I sort of start the sentence in my head but nothing comes. I think, *why I'm here is...* again nothing. I think seriously of telling her that if I knew why I was here, I mean really knew enough about myself and my mixed up emotions and guilt and grief and crippling loss, if I understood even a hint of my own cognitive processes, well, I. . . I've lost my train of thought. Okay, I think, I'm pretty sure my ability to process information like a normal human being is gone. Comprehension, inference, and desire have flown the coop. All my keen thinking skills went poof. I'm half convinced I've got selective amnesia, if there is such a thing. I don't remember a thing that matters to me before my babies came along and started growing inside me, giving me hope that someday I'd become a mother. One of those good moms that all the kids on the block love to visit and track mud across the carpet and raid the fridge and sneak a handful of Ding Dongs out of the pantry when the mom pretends to look the other way. I'm that kind of mom. When I've had enough I shoo all the neighbor kids away and it's just me and mine, two precious little boys who love me and want nothing more than to tell me about their day. Mine are a couple of boys who tell their mother everything, even the stuff they shouldn't but can't help themselves when I lay on a smile that says, "Go on. I'm your mother and you can tell your mother everything".

I don't tell Pam any of that.

I say, "I feel lost."

"Lost," Pam says and already I'm disappointed. Secretly I longed for a quick fix, a word or two of counselor-lingo that snapped me out of this stupendously bad mood.

"I can't think of a better word," I say.

"Well," Pam says and lets it hang there with no intention of saying more.

I squirm in my chair. "Where do we start?" I ask.

"Why don't we start with lost?"

I glance around the room. "It's nice," I say. "Small and comfortable." Now that I think of it the place looks like an office where you might go to get a discount mortgage.

"How long has it been, since you lost the babies," she says.

"I couldn't do what you do, listen to people's problems all day long."

"Let's talk about you."

"I almost didn't find the place. I think I was looking for a …" I'm about to say a real doctor's office but stop myself.

Pam stares at me and takes a deep breath. She blinks. I blink back. I'm stalling and she knows it. I've changed my mind. I don't want to be here. I don't want to tell anyone my problems. I don't want to know what's wrong with me.

"How long's it been?" Pam asks.

"You really want to hear this?"

"How long?"

"I'm sure my story's nothing special."

"How long?"

"Four weeks," I say. Then I tell her about the whole ugly ordeal.

At one point Pam says, "If I hear you correctly, you say you almost died."

"I did," I say, "almost die, I mean."

"Is that accurate or is the statement a tad melodramatic?"

"Melodramatic?" I'm upset she even asked.

"Exaggerated," she says.

"Exaggerated?"

"In times of stress, it's not uncommon for people to overstate. You know, maybe embroider a story or two with little flourishes."

"I don't embroider," I tell her. "If anything I do the opposite."

"How do you mean?" she asks.

"I condense. I summarize. I don't know if I forget the details or if I block out all the bad parts, but I'm certain I don't embroider. I had this horrible thing happen to me, the infection, the C-section and all the rest of it. I almost died. That much I remember. Now I just want to make some sense of it. I was pregnant. I was happy. I had happy thoughts. Now it's all gone."

"It's gone," she says.

Pam is doing her best but her habit of repeating the last few words of my sentences is growing tiresome. "I'm not sure I can get pregnant again," I say. "My doctors don't know how much damage was done, or if they do they're not telling."

"You want to get pregnant again?"

"I do."

"You do?"

"I do. I want to get pregnant." I think about my own words. I say, "I do."

"Right now, how do you feel?"

"You mean like this instant or like—"

"This instant."

"I feel empty."

"Ah huh."

Also I feel grumpy and cold and achy and my butt hurts from sitting on this stiff chair. My mind wanders and I think about what I want for lunch—a chicken guacamole sandwich at the deli over on Nicholas Lane or one of those yummy giant cupcakes from the bakery on Main. The cupcakes make me think of birthday parties and kids running round with pointed hats and confetti horns. The chicken makes me think of cute little baby chicks. Even the guacamole sort of reminds me of baby crap, but in a good way. I'm way past depressed and have recently begun thinking of myself as incurable, as though someone has thrown sand in my chemistry. Incurable or not, I shy away from medications of any kind. Even if Pam did offer me a little something to set my tidy biological syndrome on the straight and narrow, (which she doesn't, and can't), I'd refuse. I silently practice refusing. "No thank you. I'm not into drugs, even for my own good." And "I'm quite happy with my serotonin levels just where they are, thank you." And, "Why take a mood stabilizer and miss all this fun?"

The worst part of whatever indefinable thing is smothering me is that I feel alone. And being along makes me sad. And being sad makes me long for the days when I wasn't.

"How do you and your husband get along?" Pam asks.

"I love my husband," I say.

"That's not what I asked."

I scratch at a gummy spot on the arm of my chair with my fingernail. Then I sit straighter and put on a happy face and think positive thoughts. "I know," I say, "but it's the best answer I can give you."

We sit there and stare at each other, both of us wondering where to take the conversation from here.

I see Pam once a week for several weeks and in all that time, I don't give up much of the real good stuff. Go figure why someone would go to the trouble of seeing a counselor and then hold back, but that's what I do. What I should have said is that I'm a good person and I can prove it. I should have told her about my three best friends: Renee, Lisa, and Tonya. I don't know why friends come to mind, but they do, and in hindsight my friendships might be more telling of me than reciting what I think of as the "baby story," an event I only half remember because through much of it I was drugged, delirious, or both. I don't know how other people wade through a crisis like this, but me, I lean on my husband and when I feel him beginning to sag, I shift some of the burden to my three closest friends. I should have told Pam about Renee, Lisa, and Tonya and how we met, how much each of them mean to me, and how we talk on the phone every day (really).

I'm in one of those moods. I'm tired of being depressed. I want to laugh and I want to make Pam laugh. Maybe I'll give her something to smile about.

Chapter Eleven

What I Found

·····································

After high school, I enrolled at New York City's hotshot college for design and fashion, F.I.T., the Fashion Institute of Technology. My parents barely scrabbled together enough hard currency for the tuition, so it was up to me to come up with cash for food, subway fare, and anything else I need. I snagged a job at Lerners New York, a semi-hip, semi-budget clothing store for women, as a "fit model." I got the job it turned out, because I was the perfect shape, perfect size, and the perfect height. Lucky me, I was the perfect fit.

By day, I donned tops, sweaters, and pairs of pants, one after another, and pranced round a room crowded with racks of clothes and people staring at every crease, wrinkle and bulge on my body. By night I zoomed off to F.I.T. for a class on textile design, fragrance marketing, or draping techniques. At the end of the day I made the hour-long slog home to my parents' house, ate, studied and got some sleep so the next day I could do it all over again.

I loved my life.

The job was an ideal career-starter for a girl who adored clothes, design, and color and who dreamed of someday becoming a professional buyer.

I wasn't there long when the vice president of merchandising, Bob, saw hidden potential in me. He told Maggie, one of the buyers, to show me the ropes. Soon I was an assistant buyer. The three of us went on buying trips to Los Angeles, Kansas City, and Toronto. We visited the high-end retail stores, bought whatever designs we thought we would sell in our low-end market, and shipped the items off to some budget factory in middle America to crank out knockoffs.

About the time I made buyer Maggie begged off of the year's East Asian buying excursion to Hong Kong, Thailand, Taiwan, and Korea, and I slipped into her seat. That first night in Hong Kong Bob took me to dinner and politely taught me how to butter bread, a feat I felt I'd mastered some time ago, but what did I know?

Pam actually chuckles at this part.

We were sitting in a posh restaurant on the fourth floor of the hotel overlooking Hong Kong's glittery skyline. I reached for a fat slice of carrot-colored bread from the basket and scooped up a mound of whipped butter with my knife. The room was quiet and I heard Bob across the table grinding his molars.

"Mind if I give you a bit of advice," Bob asked. "About the bread."

"What about the bread?" I said. We *were* in Hong Kong. Maybe he was going to tell me the bread was made from exotic ingredients I wanted no part of—turtle jelly, dried shark fin, or aged quail eggs.

Bob reached for a slice of bread. "This may seem silly," he said, but used a tone that said listen up kid. He took his bread and tore off a small piece about half the size of a Chicken McNugget. "See what I'm doing here?" He wiped a smidgen of butter on the end of the half-nugget. He gave me an angling look to make sure I'm getting all this. "One piece at a time."

I glanced around at the other diners and didn't catch anyone buttering bread. I looked at Bob. "This is very helpful," I said.

"I'm not through." He put a portion of the nugget in his mouth, the end with the smudge of butter on it and chewed. The piece that makes it into his mouth was no bigger than a nickel. "That's how you butter bread."

"Oh,"

"You butter the piece that goes in your mouth. No more. No less."

I know Pam's response before she says it "So why did you tell me this story?"

"I don't know. I thought it was funny."

"Why of all the stories, you chose to tell this one?"

"I'm not sure, it was a long time ago.

"Were you embarrassed?" She pauses, because all good counselors are trained to pause just before a breakthrough. "Did you feel exposed? Maybe even humiliated?"

"I thought you'd like the story," I say.

"Why do you like it?"

"Bob was a teacher at heart. He used to quiz me about the industry – new developments, fabrics, styles, and patterns. He taught me to identify trends and to watch for fashion cycles. For weeks, he'd pontificate about hand feel, how the feel alone can sell a garment to the market, and I finally had to tell him, 'I get it. I get it.' He wasn't belittling the way some men can be, or at least, he didn't mean to be. He taught me about sourcing and which countries specialized in what. He taught me how to behave in meetings and how to talk to clients. And he taught me how to butter bread."

"You appreciated what he did for you?"

I say, "More now than I did at the time. He took me under his wing."

"Like a bird."

"Like a naive girl out in the world for the first time."

"Okay," says Pam. "So tell me this. What did you learn about yourself?"

"I don't know what you mean."

"What did that experience teach you about you?"

I think about life's gooeyness and how once a memory sticks, you can't ever get it unstuck and how Pam is after something and I honestly don't know what it is. "I can't tell you," I say.

"There's a lot you don't tell me," she says and she's right.

There is one breakthrough in my otherwise stagnant meetings with Pam.

"I'm thinking about a dog," I mention.

"A dog," Pam says.

"A little dog. Probably a Yorkshire terrier."

Pam tilts her head and stares at me. For a dizzyingly brief moment our distance disappears, as if we're getting to the good stuff, like now we're getting down to the heart of things and loony or not, I'm about to let loose some family secret, painful hurt. Of course that's not what I do.

Pam, it turns out, is a dog lover and any mention of dogs takes her to another dimension far away from crazies, depressive realists, and tawny-haired housewives with mood disorders.

"A Yorkie?" she says.

"I've had Yorkies before," I say. "That was a long time ago."

"Why?"

"Why a dog or why a Yorkie?"

"Either."

"I think it's what I need."

"You need a Yorkie?"

"We can talk about something else," I say. "You think I'm being silly."

I wait for some professional remark about coping, vulnerability, or the threat of future losses. By now it's clear I have no idea what goes on inside that slightly enlarged head of hers. Pam says, "I have Yorkies myself." This is the first time she's opened up about anything personal and while talking dogs isn't exactly personal, it's close.

I say, "Tell me about your dog."

"Dogs with an S," she says and goes on to tell me their names – Maisie and Gideon (Giddy for short) – their color, facial features, and the length of Giddy's whiskers. She tells me the dogs' bathing rituals, bathroom habits, and the toys they can't live without. She says more but I stop listening.

"I think I'm ready," I say.

Pam leans forward in her big overstuffed sidewalk chair. "Mine are teacup Yorkies, so small I can put Maisie in a coat pocket and not know she's there. Giddy doesn't like pockets."

"A teacup is exactly what I had in mind."

"I got mine from a woman up in Dover. If you're serious, you should give her a call."

I jot down the number and cut my weekly session short so I can rush home and make the pitch to Rick. But in truth, if I want a dog, he wants a dog. It's not that we only have one brain between us. It's that Rick is a man who genuinely wants to please me, a man who will sell his ratty old SUV if I ask and wrestle his own kids if they diss me (both of which he's already done), and who looks forward to changing crappy diapers in his fifties all because I want a baby. Here's a man willing to upset his life in every way if it makes me happy.

I call the breeder, Charlene, a woman with a voice that reminds me of a young Farrah Fawcett. Her tone is husky and half sexy and I imagine she's one of those save-the-world charity types who only got into the dog-breeding thing because she loves dogs. She gives me directions and the upcoming weekend, Rick and I detour to her house on our way to his brother's place for a party.

Charlene's house is hard to find. When we do set eyes on the place, Rick says, "You're kidding, right?"

The house is a doggy compound, all of it surrounded by chain link fencing, dog runs, giant unhinged gates, and maybe two zillion little dogs yapping at us as we ease up the dirt drive to the front door. The face of the house is sad and peeling.

I knock. A man answers with a beer in his hand, squints into the sun, and suppresses a burp. He's wearing a black tee shirt with a hole in the shoulder and a drawing of two pieces of bread with a green fog in between. Bold lettering under the drawing says, "Fart Sandwich." Inside,

I'm overwhelmed with the smell of dog pee, or at least I hope it's dog pee. Rick doesn't like dirt. He's trained in preventing infections and washing his hands. I imagine he doesn't like inhaling clouds of dog pee, though we've never discussed it. I involuntarily put the back of my hand over my mouth. It takes a few seconds to adjust to the smell of urine, and when I do I get a whiff of dog poo and other fragrances I can't put my finger on.

It takes a moment for my eyes to adjust, which is the perfect time for three mangy hounds to attack. Attack might be too strong a word here. Mostly the mutts just want to lick us and nibble the heel of one of my new shoes. What Rick thinks about dogs slobbering on his jeans, I can only guess. The man of the house doesn't even notice the dogs. He doesn't offer his name. Instead, he stares at the TV.

I see that Rick's eyes are tearing and the husband says something hilarious about the stink and laughs so hard his face turns red. He waves his beer hand gesturing at the room. "A man's home is his kennel," he says. He's talking to us but looking at the TV. We all watch a beer commercial of two women in skimpy clothes in a fistfight. "Tastes great," one says before she gets hit in the face. "Less filling," the other says as she's thrown into a public fountain and loses her blouse.

"I love this commercial," the husband says.

The top of the TV is covered in a half inch of dust and in the center of the set sits a hand painted figurine of a dog, white with black spots and a gold halo above the dog's head. I think it's a rat terrier, but I'm not sure.

"My name's Rick," my man says but doesn't offer his hand.

The husband is not susceptible to introductions. He says, "A lot of people want the big dogs, your retrievers. Your Rottweiler's." He takes a long swig of beer. "Your shepherds and what all." He scrunches up his nose acknowledging the stink in the room. To Rick, he says, "You know how much worse it'd smell around here with a litter of shepherds?"

"Not really," Rick says.

"A batch of shepherds will tear through a bag of kibble in no time and seconds later ya got yourself a landmine of shepherd shit, excuse the language. I told the wife, if we're gonna do this then it's got to be the little ones, the Shih Tzus or them mini-schnauzers. I was happy as spit when she decided on the itty-bitty Yorkies. In terms of smell I don't know that one is better than the next, but them Yorkie poops is sure a lot easier to clean up."

"Can we see the dogs?" Rick says.

"Not my job, but they're right over there if you want to take a look-see."

In the kitchen sits a makeshift pen, a combination of cardboard boxes, flattened and taped together with packing tape, parts of an old baby crib, and a couple of heavy wooden planks that might have come from a waterbed.

The woman of the house, Charlene, emerges from a back hallway. "This here is our new litter," she says looking down into the pen. This is not Farrah Fawcett standing before me.

The puppies are no bigger than tennis balls with legs. They are adorable. I lean into Rick and whisper, "I want the smallest one. That one." To Charlene I say, "Are they all available?"

"That one there is taken," Charlene, says. Her husband in the other room burps or farts, I can't tell which with any certainty, and then laughs and says something unintelligible. "And not that one," she says, "the other one there is up for grabs."

"This one," I say bending over the cardboard wall and touching one of the puppies. "It's available?"

"That's what I said."

"Is it a girl?"

"Through and through."

"She's a beautiful dog." I lift her. She's the size of a small stapler. I put her close to my face and listen to the sound her little body makes.

"What about this one?" Rick says. He bends and lifts his own dog.

"That one there's a boy," Charlene says.

The beer-drinker yells from the couch. "Watch out for them boys. They'll get you in trouble every time."

I glance at Charlene who shrugs.

"Do you mind if I ask how much?" Rick says pointing at my dog.

"Ask away," she says.

We stare at Charlene waiting for more.

Rick says, "Okay, how much?"

We go to the party and spend several hours in a corner conferring about dogs. Once we tally the vote, I call Charlene and give her the good news. We want the girl. "Uh uh," she says. I spend twenty minutes negotiating the price down to 1,600 dollars. "Cash," Charlene says. I tell her we don't have that much cash on us and she says the first one through the door with cash gets the dog. We hit the first ATM we see and make a beeline to Charlene's.

I buy the fanciest dog bag I can find, a pebble leather carrier designed to look like an upscale handbag. The perfect incognito disguise for sneaking my new dog named Beautee into restaurants, movies, and just about everywhere I go. The bag has rollback flaps, mesh ventilation windows, a place to stick her head out, and an internal leash just in case. I take my little two-and-a-half-pounder with me everywhere and nobody's the wiser.

Here is this tiny, defenseless dog that needs my help to eat, pee, get her hair done, and visit the vet. She's so small she can't even jump up on the couch without help. Without me, Beautee can't survive, or so I tell myself. A dog isn't a child. I know this. I really do. A dog is a living, breathing creature that survives on water, protein, and love. Mostly love, in my opinion. So here's the thing: I have love leaking out of my pours and no one who needs it. Rick is a grown man, for crying out loud, and while he needs love, he's doing just fine without the extra attention.

In the five months I was pregnant, I'd been stockpiling love. I'd been hoarding the stuff like a black marketer. I'd bring it to the surface, examine it, nurture it, and then stuff it away deep inside me ready to let it loose the moment my babies arrive. Only that day never came. All that bottled up love is still inside me and it needs an outlet. And as dumb as it sounds, this little teacup Yorkie of mine is that outlet.

It was Pam who gave me Beautee. And it was Beautee who gave me back my life.

One night, I sit on the couch reading a magazine and holding Beautee in my lap. Rick sits across from me for a time, not speaking but watching us, the way I involuntarily reach over and stroke Beautee's head or scoot her closer to me, folding myself into a pillow to make her more comfortable. He watches me let her chew on the piping of a new diamond quilted accent pillow for a moment longer than I should before I scold her and politely ask her to promise not to do it again.

He says, "Does this mean you don't want to try again?"

He means, of course, that I appear so happy with Beautee here in my lap that it's possible I've lost all interest in a real flesh-and-blood baby to hold, snuggle, and care for. From the other side of the coffee table, I might ask the same thing. Within days of bringing Beautee home, my funk lifts. In two weeks, I'm a new woman. I answer the phone when it rings and shower every day and put on makeup without complaining. I walk the length of the house and remember why I bothered. I stop mumbling. The sun is brighter and clearer and the gray days aren't nearly as gray. Losing the twins has stripped away some part of me and exposed a raw hurt I'd never felt before. And that miserable experience has done something else to me. In surviving it made me more determined than ever.

"I want to try again," I say. Rick looks at Beautee as I give her a kiss. "OK," he says.

Chapter Twelve

In Vitro Two and Three

···

I n June, two months after losing the twins, I make the trek into Baltimore to see Dr. Griffin. The big question is when we start the next *in vitro* fertilization cycle. Dr. Griffin has large hands and eyes that dart around the bare exam room. I realize that he's better at the mechanics of medicine than addressing the gooey intangibles of patient feelings. He nods at me and studies my chart. "Are you sure you're up for this?"

"I want a child," I say.

"That's not exactly what I asked."

The two of us stare at each other, as if waiting for the other to flinch. Being married to one, I've learned that doctors seldom flinch. I look away and say, "I'd like to get started as soon as possible. Now, suits me fine."

"We can't do anything until you've healed."

"I'm healed."

"No you're not. Not really." There's something on his mind, I can tell. What exactly, he's not giving up. "It's tentative," he says, "but I don't see any reason we can't initiate the next cycle in September."

"Then September it is," I say.

I decided to leave my job, to be free of bosses, clients, and road trips to Pennsylvania and New Jersey. No more arguing over who sold what and to whom. But what to do next with my life? Of course I have the next IVF cycle to look forward to which is always a thrill—taking meds that make me crazy or at a minimum no fun to be around; stabbing myself with giant, spear-like needles filled with fertility potions guaranteed to give me hot flashes, sore breasts, oh, and ripen my eggs; and the always fun spread-your-legs-and-let-us-reach-inside-there-for-a-little-egg-retriving procedure. I mull over my options—re-paint the kitchen, weed the flower beds in front, wash my car—anything to take my mind off that I'm forty going on ninety. Time is running out.

In the end, I decide to volunteer for the Big Brother Big Sister program. I want to do something important, something real, tangible, meaningful. Helping a wayward little girl seems the perfect solution. At the same time I hope to distract myself, to get my mind off losing the twins, something I'm getting better at but have not yet perfected. I look up the Big Brothers' organization on the Internet, review the site with its bright colors and all the stories of men and women hooking up with parentless kids and making a difference. Once I get my own little girl to sponsor, the site says, we get to shoot hoops, play board games, hike, eat pizza, and learn to cook Latin dishes like aspopao—a dish that resembles meatloaf, but with chicken. In late June I visit the local Big Brothers Big Sisters' office in Georgetown, about fifteen miles away, where I talk to a woman who eyes me carefully.

She says, "Are you willing to spend at least an hour a week with a child?"

I nod and give her one of my big salesy grins, as if to say, I can't wait.

The woman puts my name on a list for "community-based mentoring" and agrees to send someone out to my home for a look. About mid-July, two women, both with earnest, hopeful faces arrive at my house. I invite them into the living room, a room Rick and I seldom use but which seems perfect for wowing Big Brothers Big Sisters' operatives into believing I can be trusted alone with a needy child. We have a nice chat and several days later I get word that I passed, and thus get the okay to proceed to step two.

The woman I first met at the office, Tasha, sends me a packet of materials and a stack of forms to fill out and return to the office. I scribble out my information and check the box that says I agree to a background check to verify, I suppose, that I'm not a perv, no felonies, no arrests for child porn, etcetera. Two weeks later, I get more good news. I'm eligible to become a Big Sister.

Now I wait.

Tasha, or some other conscientious person, sorts through the organization's database of children who need a big sister and tries to find a suitable match. Finally, I get a phone call. I've been matched with Kara, a ten-year-old girl right here in Delaware. The timing of the meet isn't clear, the woman tells me, but she's working on it. "I'll be in touch," she says.

In the meantime, Dr. Griffin schedules me for a delightful little D&C procedure, basically a process to scrape out my uterus and whisk away any of the aftereffects of my c-section. I have to go under anesthesia and therefore Dr. Griffin tells me I'll need someone with me to drive me home. I invite Tonya for the outing into Baltimore and she graciously agrees to watch over me for the day. The procedure goes smoothly and the next day I'm back to normal

Soon thereafter the good doctor gives me the green light for IVF number two. Dr. Griffin offers only four IVF cycles a year and schedules dozens of woman at the same time. Miss this one and I have to wait another three months. I only now realize that my plate is full—spending time with Rick, last minute planning for an Italian vacation we planned after our loss of the twins, managing my own emotional state, looking after Beautee, anticipating my upcoming meet up with Kara, and of course the chore of getting my own menstrual cycle in sync with the doctor's fertility cycle.

"Our next cycle begins, let's see, the end of September," Dr. Griffin says.

"I understand," I say.

"Does that mean I can pencil you in?"

"Ink," I say. "Ink me in."

"You're sure you want to do this?"

I'm well past tired of answering this question. He and I are on the phone, but I can imagine the expression on his face, the smile that never shows any teeth, and the permanent wrinkles in his forehead that give you the impression of a man holding up some invisible weight. Like a man who isn't telling all he knows.

"More than anything in my life," I say.

"You had a difficult time with your last pregnancy," he says.

"I'm healthy," I say and pause trying to think up some snappy witticism, but nothing comes. "I want to do this."

He clears his throat and plainly starts to say one thing in a meaningful doctor's voice and then changes his mind and breathes into my ear like a professional yogi, in through the nose, out through the mouth. "I'll see you end of September," he says.

I finally meet my little sister, Kara. I'm days away from beginning another round of IVF shots and mood altering medications and exams and while I try my best to put on a cheery face, deep down I'm starting to dread a repeat of the process. Not to mention not knowing how things will turn out. I consider myself an adventurous person, but making a baby via *in vitro* fertilization is not so much an adventure as an exercise of faith.

Throwing Kara into the mix, I admit, is not perfect timing. There's no telling how I'll feel this time around. Fortunately, she's local and there's no good reason we can't spend an hour or more a week together. The connection might do us both some good.

The first time we meet, I'm there with Kara, her grandmother, and Marcia, a woman from the Big Brothers Big Sisters organization, whose purpose is to chaperone and I'm honestly not sure who she's chaperoning, me or Kara.

The grandmother, Dorothea, and little Kara live in a part of our town I've never seen or knew existed. The apartment complex is a series of wood-sided boxes with warped and peeling boards, with nails backing their way out of the lumber and now sticking out like hundreds of angry little spikes. It takes a millisecond to grasp that this is no place for a woman in a baby blue convertible Mercedes. Later, when I tell Rick about the set up, he forbids me, as much as my husband forbids anything, from visiting at night.

On the passenger seat of my car is an entirely too big bouquet of flowers. I picked up the bundle at Posey Place Florist's, a cute little flower shop in town that doubles as a pet funeral service. Really. The flowers are for Dorothea. I grab the flowers, press my car's lock button, and move quickly up the chipped concrete steps to the walkway on the second floor. Kara's fretful building is two stories tall and her place is a flight up, twenty paces down a narrow walkway, second door on the left. There's absolutely no reason to be scared. So naturally, I'm way more frightened than I should be which makes me think some part of me is picking up subtle clues of unrecognized dangers. What I actually see all around me is decay, rot, and decomposition, and the evidence of an environment coming unhinged. The unhinged part is more feeling than logical assessment. I make a mental note to talk to Rick about this and by *this* I mean either that Kara lives in an icky environment or that I feel vulnerable way too often lately.

I glance behind me. No one.

I look both ways down the long walkway. No one.

I peek over the low wall into the parking lot. No one. Nothing out of the ordinary.

I knock on #213 and Dorothea answers, gives me a wave of her hand and motions me to squeeze past her, our bellies almost rubbing as I turn sideways in the tight space and shuffle to my right, flowers in hand, as Dorothea awkwardly stands her ground with one hand on the open door. Once inside, I see that the place is surprisingly clean. In one glance, I take in the kitchen, living room, hallway, and through an open door the better part of a bedroom.

"I'm so glad you made it," Dorothea says.

Her statement throws me. "Was there a question I might not?"

"No, no. I don't know what I'm saying. I'm just happy to meet you. I'm Dorothea." I open my mouth but Dorothea interrupts. "I can't believe it. Here you are. I don't know what I expected."

She shuffles into the small kitchen and there's a hitch in her step as if some combination of bones in the spine-hip-pelvis region is catching on something it shouldn't. She moves in a jerky, bouncy way that creates a rhythm all her own.

On the couch facing a bulky faux-wooden cabinet that holds the television sits Marcia, the chaperone, a woman with a soft face and her hair pulled back behind her ears. The hairdo looks intentional, as if the bylaws of Big Brothers Big Sisters chaperoning are clear on this point: appropriate appearance for site visits is competent and concerned, which Marcia pulls off like a real pro.

Marcia stands. "Let me get Kara," she says without introducing herself.

Kara is apparently in her room and refuses to come out. I know this because I can hear Marcia, and then Dorothea, charming the girl, then goading, and finally threatening her in subtle ways I can't hear but nonetheless sense. Finally out she comes.

"Hi," I say.

"Hi," Kara says from the hallway and even in this simple two-letter word I can tell this little girl is a bit slow. Not severely or even permanently confused, but unaware. She's not nervous or tentative the way most ten-year-olds might be meeting someone new. She stares directly at me, smiles, and waits for whatever comes next.

"Well," I say.

Kara glances away from me to the TV, which is on with the sound turned low. On the screen is a wide pasture filled with cows, the cows' lips moving, apparently talking to each other about a couple of tourists. The cows appear to be laughing. Kara giggles.

"It's a pleasure to meet you," I say.

Kara smirks at me and turns back to the television.

"I'm not sure what we do from here," I say. This is a ploy. I'm leaving an opening for Kara to suggest something, anything. I realize I know next to nothing about what children think about, and even less about what goes on in the minds of little girls who live in tiny apartments with their grandmothers.

Kara thinks about my question for a half second and opens her mouth to speak only Dorothea gets there first. She says, "Why don't you show Mrs. Simons your room?"

"Sharon," I say.

"Okay then. Take Sharon and let her see your drawings."

"You like to draw?" I ask Kara.

"She does," Dorothea says. "You'll see."

Kara doesn't move.

"What do you draw?" I ask.

"Lots of things," Dorothea says. "She's been waiting to show you. Go on," she says to Kara and reaches over and gives the little girl a push on the shoulder to get her going.

Kara looks down the hall at her bedroom door and then back to the TV, now showing a commercial of two cavemen eating dinner at a fancy restaurant. I know this commercial. I can't actually hear the words, but that doesn't matter. It's the caveman's tone and sarcasm that makes the commercial funny. I can't help it. I laugh. "Do you like this commercial?" I ask Kara.

"We both do," Dorothea says.

Dorothea hovers over the little girl as if Kara is a delicate porcelain doll. Treat her too roughly, ask a difficult question, make her think on her own, and she might crack. I'm tempted to tell Dorothea to put a lid on it, give the girl a little time to formulate a sentence or two. The next thirty minutes is pretty much more of the same—me asking questions designed to get Kara to open up, or at a minimum to say something, and Dorothea answering for her. At some point I realize these two have been communicating in this way for a long time. It's become more than habit; it's a reflex.

Marcia lounges in a chair, circa 1970s accent chair covered in a captain's wheel pattern. For thirty minutes, she doesn't take her eyes off me.

I visit the apartment just that once.

For meeting number two, I drive into the parking lot where Kara is waiting for me by the stairs. She climbs in my car, and we zoom off without so much as a word from Dorothea. I take Kara over to our house. She is overwhelmed with the volume of it, the number of rooms, the tile floors and wood trim and all the windows looking out onto our back yard, the size of a small park, and the river flowing by.

We're standing in the kitchen when she says, "Where am I going to live?"

"Honey," I say, "that's not part of the plan."

I pause, thinking just how best to say whatever it is I plan to say when she says, "Okay, but which is my room?"

"Kara, sweetheart, this is my home. You can visit anytime you want, but you have your own home."

"I know."

"You live with your grandmother."

"I know," she says and I think I'm getting somewhere. Then she says, "But I get my own room, right?"

"Why don't we go for a bike ride?"

In the garage, I move some boxes out of the way and we get a good look at three slightly dusty bicycles, leftovers from Rick's kids.

Kara says, "I get my own bike?"

What she needs most is my patience.

Tasha, my contact at Big Brothers Big Sisters, makes me swear on a stack of aging manila file folders not to spoil the girl. I'm warned repeatedly not to make our visits about money. Don't pay for our friendship with cash, gifts, or toys of any kind, which I soon realize is harder than it sounds. I like buying what I want, but with Kara in tow, and Tasha's stern warnings ringing in my ears, I feel guilty each time I even think of forking over a dollar to buy Kara a pack of gum. The Big Sister experience is certainly different and challenging, both frustrating and gratifying. I hope I'm helping her.

On October 30, I begin the IVF protocol again. First, I slap on a birth control patch. A few days later, I begin poking myself with shots. In truth, Rick does most of the poking because he's better at it than I am given that I have my eyes shut most of the time. Evening and morning for weeks, Rick fills up a syringe the size of a water bottle and squirts me full of Lupron and follicle stimulating hormone, HCG, and a little progesterone for good measure. I have toughened and the needles don't seem to bother me as much anymore. At the same time, I begin regular visits to the doctor's office in Baltimore, rising every few days at five-thirty and lumbering through Baltimore traffic in time to make my eight a.m. appointment.

Once again, the meds catch up with me and send my emotions into hyper drive. I see a puppy in a television commercial and I cry. Or I see some minor injustice, say a six-year-old pushing a five-year-old around, and I want to wring that six-year-old's neck. The old, naturally calm me is gone and I can't help thinking the former me is gone forever. Intellectually I know it doesn't make any sense, that what I think and feel in this moment aren't necessarily real, but that understanding doesn't change a thing. I float from despair to elation in the time it takes to read a sentence in the newspaper. Sometimes it just zooms straight to despair. And still others, my emotions do the bunny-hop—elation, despair, euphoria, despair, wariness with a dash of hopelessness.

In just three days I rediscover my zeal for starting arguments.

"You said you'd be home at seven," I say to Rick as he saunters into the kitchen at quarter to eight.

"Did I?" he says. He stops and gives me his full attention, his mouth slightly open and his eyes in a squint, trying his hardest to recall what exactly he did say, if anything.

In truth, I can't remember what he said or if I just expected him at seven and he didn't meet my expectations. "You did," I say. "You said seven." I'm tempted to spell it out S-E-V-E-N, but catch myself.

"Well then, I'm sorry. I had a patient who needed my help."

"Is this your way of saying you'd rather be at work than home with me? Because if it is, I'll just leave you to it. Is that what you want? You want me to go in the other room and pretend I'm not here?"

"I think you're over reacting."

"Is that so? I ask for one thing, that you keep your word, and you think that's asking too much is it?"

"I'm a few minutes late." Rick turns sideways looking for any signs of food preparation, any hint that he might get something to eat anytime soon. "I'm pretty sure I didn't say seven. For the life of me, I don't remember us talking about it at all."

"So now I'm making it up?"

"I didn't say that."

Tears begin to well in my eyes.

"Honey," he says, "I love you. Let's go in the living room and sit and talk."

Rick knows how to handle me. He's been down this road. He now knows all about the side effects of fertility medications, and the zany, irrational things that can go through my head during this process. In November, I trek to the hospital for more testing. This I do on the seventh, the ninth, eleventh, and again on the thirteenth. Then egg retrieval day arrives. I have to go under anesthesia, so I need a clear-thinker to drive me home after the procedure. Rick is booked solid with patients. He half offers to reschedule but it seems unfair to all the people who need his help. Tonya is busy with some I-can't-reschedule family happening. I call Dr. Griffin's nurse and ask just how out-of-it I'll be after the retrieval. She giggles into the phone and then clears her throat and does her best to make me understand that I *must* be accompanied by a licensed driver. If I don't have someone to drive me home, don't show up for the procedure.

I think long and hard about what to do. Then I call Dorothea and ask her if she knows anyone who might be willing to chauffer me around for the day. "I'll pay," I say.

"How much?" Dorothea asks.

"I hadn't gotten that far."

"It's a long drive to Baltimore and back."

"It is," I say.

"And then a lot of sitting around in the hospital."

"More than you think," I tell her. "I'll be in recovery at least a couple of hours after."

"And the drive home again. That's a long day."

"For all of it," I say, "300 dollars."

"In cash?"

"However."

"Okay, I'll do it," she says.

Somewhere in the conversation she tells me about an unpaid electric bill I had a suspicion I might be covering with or without the chauffeuring duties. In a way, I feel I'm helping, like I'm doing Dorothea a favor and not the other way around.

On Thursday, I climb into Rick's new SUV, back out of the garage and lumber over to pick up Dorothea. It's five a.m. and cold outside. When I pull up to the apartment building I see Dorothea and sleepy-eyed Kara standing beside the stairs waiting for me. Lugging Kara along wasn't part of the plan, but here we are.

"You sure you're okay with this?" I say to Dorothea.

"Yes, of course," she says.

"I want to be sure, because they won't release me if I don't have someone with me to drive home."

"Yes, yes, I understand."

I reach into my purse and pull out two hundreds and five twenties. I count it and hand it to Dorothea. "Let's get this out of the way. I'm not sure how I'll feel after the procedure."

"You're a godsend," she says and stuffs the money in her purse.

"You sure you can drive?"

"I've been driving longer than you've been alive."

At the hospital, I go through the procedure. The anesthesia wears off, sort of, and I'm paroled early for good behavior, though I'm groggy and have a royal stomachache. The nurse shows me the wheelchair. I sit, and Kara pushes me to the hospital glass doors where I stand and wave to the nurse. The three of us aim for the SUV in the parking lot. We find it and I shuffle around to the passenger side. Dorothea stands there in front of the truck. She says, "I can't drive."

Even with a slightly addled brain, I'm pretty sure I heard what she said. "I don't understand," I say.

"Not today," Dorothea says and looks off across the parking lot.

"I thought we talked about this?"

"The truck," she touches the chrome grill of the big SUV with the tips of her arthritic fingers, "it's too much for me to handle. Some other time, perhaps."

Dorothea pats the hood and looks back over her shoulder at the hospital building and the glass doors. She parts her lips and I see her crooked teeth. I want to say something about her teeth. I want it to hurt, to humiliate Dorothea in some meaningful way and that also makes my achy stomach pains go away. I do no such thing, of course. I put my own hand on a fender and say, "Another time?"

"I'll let you decide. Anytime is good for me."

"Right now is a good time."

"I mean another time," she says intentionally ignoring my desperate attitude. "You can tell me all about the . . ." she doesn't know what to call it, a truck, a car, an SUV, "somewhere with not too many cars around and I can practice my turns."

My stomach hurts. My head throbs, but not bad enough to see stars. I think I'm thinking clearly, or clear enough to drive us the 131 miles back to the Blue Hen State without running any stoplights or smashing us head-on into a trucker hauling soybeans. "Fine," I say in a soft voice. "Hop in."

I walk around to the driver's side, step up into the SUV, buckle up and turn and smile at Kara in the back seat. I crank the key. It feels hard and awkward in my hand.

During the two-hour slog home, Dorothea tells me how she and Kara are struggling. "Financially," she says just in case my brain isn't running on all cylinders. To make her point, she unbuckles, always an unwise decision when the driver is partially sedated, and wrenches her body around to look at Kara and give the little girl an exaggerated head nod. I can't see Kara's reaction, but I assume she nods back, as if to say, "Yep, we're struggling. Financially." Thankfully we arrive home intact. I've had quite enough of Dorthea, being duped when I'm vulnerable does not go over very well with me.

Days later, Rick and I return to the hospital for implantation. The procedure goes well and for the next two weeks, we anxiously wait for news. A nurse rings me at home and says that my whatever level is at 104, a definitive sign that I'm pregnant. I wait until Rick gets home from work to tell him. We hug. We are happy, but we know this is only one of many steps in a process with oodles of steps and not a single guarantee. We've already been bitten with disappointment, like gamblers who bet on a sure thing only to have their horse stumble out of the gate and lose. IVF number two is a big gamble, but at least we're out of the gate and running. Rick grabs a beer from the fridge, a water for me, and we sit at the kitchen table and talk. I ask about his day. He asks how I feel. I sip my bottled water and think of all the things that can go wrong.

"I feel great," I say.

"I love you," he says.

"I know."

Two days later my HCG levels are up again. I'm still pregnant, the nurse says, but there's little optimism in her voice. My level of human chorionic gonadotropin isn't going up fast enough. She schedules me for an appointment with Dr. Griffin, a bad sign. The doctor sits me down and gives me the sickening news straight away. It's a tubal pregnancy. An ectopic pregnancy, he calls it. My egg is growing outside the womb and can't survive. The doctor gives me about eight seconds to let the news sink in and tells me to talk to the nurse on my way out and schedule another appointment. For several long days, I look forward to a shot of methotrexate, a powerful drug used to treat cancer, as well as dissolve unruly pregnancies. On schedule Rick and I arrive at his hospital's outpatient clinic. In the exam room I pull down my pants and the nurse says, "This is going to hurt."

"Okay," I say.

"It's one of the most painful shots we administer."

I love the lingo nurses use. Administer. Intramuscular. Gluteal muscles.

She says, "I'll do my best to be gentle. Roll over a bit. That's it. I'll inject you here in the outer quadrant of the buttock." She touches my butt with a gloved finger. "Ready?"

"Do I have a choice?"

And she sticks me. She's a woman of her word. The stick is like nothing I have felt in months. Painful and slow and I don't move a muscle for fear I'll have to do it all over again. It hurts and my eyes water and I want to scream at someone. She yanks the needle out of me and I half expect to hear a cork-popping noise. I pull up my pants and wipe my eyes and stand to leave.

The next day my butt is still sore. "Anything I can do to help?" Rick asks.

"I'm so sad and disappointed I don't think there's much you can do right now. Maybe I'll try to take my mind off things and go shopping for Christmas presents", I say.

I call Tasha at Big Brothers Big Sisters for one of my regular check-ins, and since Christmas is fast approaching Tasha reminds me again, the program is about connecting kids with healthy, well-adjusted adults. It's about connection. It's about spending time together. It's about enriching each other's lives. It's not about money, so go easy on the Christmas presents.

In any event, Dorthea already told me some of what Kara wants, a pair of earrings. I don't want to mess this up—get the long pretty ones versus the circular cute ones—so I decide to give her a gift card to Target instead. It's not about the money, I remind myself. It's about connection, I tell myself. Left to my own devises, I'd probably buy her a car or a year's tuition at Wesley College or some other ridiculously expensive gift. I control the urge to give away the farm and I buy a gift card for fifty dollars. A few days after Christmas, I visit Dorothea and Kara and I hand over the card.

"That's it?" Dorothea says. She takes the card from Kara and stares at it, inspecting the Target logo, rubbing it with her finger as if there might be something hidden underneath there.

"Well," I say.

"Fifty?" she says.

"That's right."

"Fifty dollars?" she says again. "It's hard to imagine what sort of present you can buy nowadays for fifty dollars." She hands the card to Kara and says, "It's not like we aren't grateful. Don't think we're not. We are, really, we are. It's just, you know, I was thinking of something more substantial."

"Like how substantial?" I ask.

"You all live in that big house. You drive nice cars. I just thought you wouldn't mind giving a little girl a Christmas she wouldn't forget."

"Uh uh."

"You're mad."

"You mentioned substantial."

"I shouldn't have said anything."

No she shouldn't. But that's not what's bugging me.

The thing is I agree with Dorothea. We are both on the same side of this one, yet I find myself defending a position that stinks. At the same time *I am* angry with her. I'm irked she isn't happy for the fifty. I half expected her to gush over the card and promise to buy Kara a pair of earrings she'd really like. Here's what else is bugging me: I love Christmas. I love giving. I love kids and grandmothers. So why do I feel so miserable? The aborted pregnancy, the driving fiasco and semi-arguments with Dorothea, the sad look on Kara's face when I give her the card. I've had enough. A few days later, I call the agency and tell them I'm through.

Shortly after Christmas, Tonya and I meet for lunch at a restaurant in Delaware. I haven't seen her in some time and I've forgotten how beautiful and fit she is; brown hair, a toothy bristling smile, that trim body of hers that makes me want to hate her if I had it in me.

"Look," Tonya says. "I want to ask you something, but I don't know how you'll take it."

"What?" I say. Feeling uncomfortable, I push my silverware to one side and look around the restaurant for anyone I might recognize.

"I feel weird saying this," she says. She follows my glance and turns and looks over her shoulder and then back at me. She has my full attention. "Well, okay," she says. "I'll just say it."

"I wish you would."

"If you want, I can have the baby for you. In vitro, whatever it takes, I'm up for it if it makes you happy."

I fiddle with my fork and wait for some hidden message to surface, some not-so-funny punch line that evades me at the moment. The medications are still sluicing through my body causing all sorts of odd side effects one of which is that I cry at odd, uneventful moments. This, on the other hand, is an eventful moment. For nearly a minute I stare at the tabletop and can't muster a tear. Then it begins and I feel a gusher coming on. "What are you saying?"

"Forget it. Bad idea, I can see that. I should have known better."

Tonya is my best friend. In the last several months our relationship has flourished. She knows how much I want a child, to be a mother. In a way she feels guilty, though she's never said so. Tonya is fertile, a regular baby-making machine while I'm not. Back when it was way funnier than it is now, we used to joke that on windy days Tonya had a good chance of catching something in the breeze and getting pregnant. And now she makes this generous but crazy offer, even though she knows what I've gone through – the potent medications, painful shots and ensuing mood swings.

Tears well in my eyes. I say, "You don't know what you're saying, what-all's involved."

"We could use your fertilized eggs, or perhaps my eggs, and go the implantation route and I'll be the surrogate. Either way I get fat for nine months and produce a baby. What's not to know?"

She's right, of course. We still have another Petri dish with a dollop of Rick's sperm frozen and squired away in some hospital refridge. "You'd do that to your body? I mean, you'd want to?"

Tonya shrugs and stares at me the way she does when she knows I'm thinking things over.

She is sweet to offer. I lift my napkin, look it over and wipe the tears from my cheeks and under my eyes. "I want to try again," I say.

"I understand. Really. I do."

"In my heart, I want to have a baby myself." I hold the soggy napkin over my heart and smile, thankful how fortunate I am to have a friend as wonderful as Tonya.

Rick and I agreed this would be our last try; emotionally, financially we are about done but still have hope since our IVF has taken twice in the past, so it has to take this third time. It has to. No reason it won't take a third time. I'm wrong, of course. There are lots of reasons it won't take, but that doesn't stop me from going forward. In March, Rick and I visit Dr. Griffin and I start IVF cycle number three—patch, stimulation meds, check ups, egg retrieval, fertilization, and implantation. The doctor slips three healthy fertilized eggs deep inside me and I wait two weeks to hear if I'm pregnant.

I'm not.

It's over. We tried and we failed. Three strikes and we're out. Disappointment, sadness, and frustration follow but for some reason, way down deep inside I still believe I am going to be a mom.

It's said when one door closes, another may open, and that door just may have opened between IVF #2 and IVF #3.

Chapter Thirteen

Adoption

I n January on a shockingly cold morning before IVF #3 began, I
had sat on the couch, laptop poised for action on my outstretched
legs, and googled the word "adoption." The little caption under the
search bar indicated 90,000 results, wow. During the past several weeks
a little voice inside my head had been whispering to me. I couldn't tell
if it was the kind of murmur a sane person should pay attention to or
the sort that required the attention of a big-eared psychiatrist. The voice
whispered, "In vitro isn't working." It said, "If you really want a baby,
try something else." Sometimes the voice asked a question. "Have you
considered adoption?"

The answer was sort of. I'd thought of adoption, but only as a far
off alternative to popping out a baby on my own. The on-my-own part
didn't seem to be working, so there I was with 90,000 clicks ahead of me.
Many of the adoption stories I scanned were cautionary tales – what could
go wrong, how long the process could take, just how bad things could
get – that sort of thing. Adoption chat rooms were filled with consoling
voices about post-adoption disasters, mangled family relationships, and
the need for some good, old fashioned crisis planning. Others gave advice

about why not to fall in love with the photo, about baby naming, and about dealing with a reluctant spouse. Most of the guidance centered on being patient. As in "You've waited this long, so what's the rush?" Get used to waiting, these women said in a thousand different ways. One lady waited two years for a beautiful, happy-faced baby from China. The more I read, the more anxious I felt. Maybe we were too late. Maybe all the babies were gone. I felt like a buyer. I wanted a baby and I wanted it now. The supply was dwindling I told myself, the demand expanding, the market for babies getting smaller and smaller and I was going to be left with nothing. I felt rushed to take action, any action so long as I was moving forward.

The requirements for adoption were arduous. I read about legal criteria, agency criteria, birth parent rights, adopting parent limitations, marital status, length of marriage, age of adoptive parents, health issues, and on it went. On a nippy day in January, I stumbled across an international adoption agency, and gave them a ring. I asked about the adoption process and listened to a sweet woman's voice rattle off a somewhat rehearsed spiel about filling out an application and was reminded, not once but three times, to insert a crisp 500 dollar check with my response. In the meantime, I was told, I may as well get on with the home study. Although in my heart I felt IVF #3 was going to work, I knew having a backup plan is what I needed.

An adoption home study is basically a paperwork nightmare required by state law. An organization in good favor with the state gets the pleasure of nosing into your background, thumbing through your health records, sniffing your income statements for anything smelly, and furrowing a brow at your autobiographical statement (the sort of statement that, if you're anything like me, took hours to craft and in the end doesn't resemble the real you in any way). As unattractive as the process is, if you want to adopt, you don't have a choice.

I schedule the home study with a woman from a nearby agency. My first chore is to fill out yet another mound of forms and immediately there's a hitch—Rick and I haven't been married quite long enough. So we do what any well educated and slightly stubborn parents would do in this situation: we bend the truth. In the blank for length of marriage, I list our relationship as lasting years before we decided to marry rather than a year. After two IVF procedures and a third upcoming, two failed pregnancies, and a near death experience, it feels like years. Ms. McKee, our rep, who sounds all of twelve on the phone, gives me a hint of what's to come, most involving fees: application fee, biometric fee (huh?), home study fee, in-country fee, placement agency fee, travel expenses, visa and medical visa fees, post placement fees, attorney fees, etcetera. As part of the home study, Rick and I must meet with Ms. McKee separately. I go first and the experience isn't all that bad (and yes, Ms. McKee looks about twelve as well). Rick has an appointment a week later. As he prepares to leave the house, I ask, "Are you nervous?"

"Should I be?"

"Just please don't screw this up."

Rick wants to say something but pauses and takes a deep breath. "I'm a professional," he says finally, a bit smugly for my taste.

"Is that supposed to comfort me?"

"I'll call you after and let you know how things went."

"I'm not saying you will."

"I know." His voice is soft and he grins at me, somehow knowing this small gesture puts me at ease.

"It's just, well, this is important to me."

"I know."

He jingles the keys in his hand and marches off down the hall and into the garage.

He apparently passes the Ms. McKee test, if it was a test, because a week later she shows up at our house with clipboard in hand, ready to count bedrooms and baths and give us the A-okay on a kid-friendly environment. She marches from room to room, making scribbly cryptic notes on her clipboard. The whole thing takes about ten minutes.

In February, still waiting to start IVF #3, I decide to go back to work. There are lots of reasons to get back in the game – to keep my mind off babies, IVF, and adoption – but the real reason is to show Rick's kids I'm not a mooch (just in case they were thinking I was). I'd supported myself my entire life and a job was part of my make-up. Rick and I don't need the money, exactly, but that doesn't mean I wouldn't like a purse-full of my own, as a result of my efforts.

The first thing I do is rummage through my old black book of contacts. I stop when I come across a familiar name, Tim. Back in the day, he was an insurance agent whom I called on when I peddled workers' compensation insurance. I heard through the grapevine that he recently had started his own company selling insurance to homeowners in four counties along the coast. The coastal homeowners market is a specialty market in that very few underwriters cover homes in an area where a pesky hurricane every ten years or a summer storm can trigger millions in claims and force even the healthiest insurance company into the red.

I call Tim and we chat some before he reads my mind. When he offers me a job, I say yes without so much as a "What's it pay?" We agree I'll work two full days a week from home or on the road, and he'll pay me by the day. No benefits. No vacation days. No boss looking over my shoulder. If things go well, at the end of the year I'll receive a bonus check in the mail. I start the following week and the transition is a cinch. I make a bunch of calls, explain the product, and answer questions. If an agent is interested, I sign him up, teach him the online system, and move on to the next agent on my list. What's not to love?

The first month, I sign up several new agents. The following month several more, and I'm off and running. But all I can think about is becoming a mom.

The home study interviews are behind us but we are a long way from the finish line. I had been fingerprinted prior to my short stint as a Big Sister, but now Rick and I have the joy of being printed by the FBI. Next, we review our options. We nix a domestic adoption because I have this slightly irrational feeling that my child's biological parents will show up years in the future and steal my child away from me. In my mind, said child is now seven or eight when it happens, upstairs tugging on his Little

League outfit where he is pitching in the first game of the playoffs. My vision deteriorates from here, but the incident is a disaster no matter how you cut it. (And without my son on the mound, his team loses the game.) I've read horror stories of just such happenings and true or not, after all I've been through I'm scared silly of loving a child and then losing him to imaginary people.

So if not here, then where?

It's now March. After receiving our paperwork I get a call from the international adoption agency politely telling us that Rick is too old to adopt an infant, though they'd be happy to offer us a six-year-old with possible attachment issues. As I shoot the agency a rash of e-mails, I learn that every agency and every country has its own rules. In Korea, you can't be obese. In Thailand, you can't be single. In Slovakia, you're required to hang out in the country while the authorities plow through the paperwork—generally about a year. In Indonesia the residency requirement is two years. I learn something else in my little give-and-take with European agencies. Prepare yourself, they e-mail me, for the long haul. A typical European adoption takes two years. Probably longer.

But still I have IVF #3.

Late in the month I find out IVF number three didn't take.

April. Rick and I talk about my desire to be a mom. At this point I feel more determined than ever, like I did when I left Paul: no one is going to stop me from being a mother, no one. But no more *in vitro*.

We turn our full attention to adoption.

Rick and I come up with a short list of possibilities. Considering all the various restrictions (including Rick's age), our search has essentially narrowed to Eastern Europe or thereabouts. I'm thinking Ukraine, maybe Russia.

May. I'm at it again surfing the Web for international adoption sites. Rick is at the hospital working, so I have the house to myself. In my clicking around, I come across an international agency based in Illinois. The site is all sky-blues and hopeful clouds and photos of children yucking it up. It also says they have children available immediately. This is around nine at night. I figure what the hell, pick up the phone and dial the number. A woman answers.

"I'm interested in adopting a baby," I say. "A Ukrainian baby. Or Russian."

"I don't normally answer the phone this late," the woman says. "Some last minute paper work, you understand."

I press on. "Is it possible, what I said about adopting a baby? Is that, well, doable?"

I listen, trying to place the woman on a scale from helpful to you're-wasting-my-time. She breathes noisily into the phone. "Have you completed your home study?"

"All behind us."

"Pardon me for asking, but how serious are you?"

"I'm not sure I understand the question."

"About adopting? Are you ready to move forward today?"

"Today?" I feel a chill sweep through my family room. I hear crackling on the other end of the line, as if I've suddenly lost some meaningful connection.

"Look," the woman says, "if I have a baby today, are you ready to say yes?"

"I am."

"Are you in front of your computer?"

"Right here on my lap."

"Hold on a sec and I'll e-mail you a photo. He's the cutest little boy you've ever seen. From east-central Russia. There, it's gone. Check your e-mail."

"What's his name?"

"Sergey."

I click on the Send/Receive button every three seconds until the file arrives. "I got it." I open the email and click on one of two photos. A toddler in a yellow and black outfit stares at me. In one photo, he has a finger in his toothless mouth and a big smile on his face. In the other, no finger, just the toothless smile. "He's beautiful," I say. "My husband and

I have been approved in our home study for two children. I was hoping for a boy and a girl."

"Okay, let me send you another photo. A girl."

When I get the photo the girl looks ill, or if not exactly ill, then not right in some way I can't put words to. Her little cheeks appear splotchy, her eyes unfocused.

"My name's Jill, by the way."

"Sorry, I'm Sharon. About the girl," I say and then run out of steam and just let my half-sentence hang there. What do I say? I want a healthy baby. Is saying so rude? Am I sifting through photos like I might a bin of bargain blouses at Bloomingdale's? "The girl," I start again, but that's all I get out.

"Don't worry about it," Jill says. "Look, give me some time to go through my records. I'll send more photos tomorrow. About Sergey, your timing is perfect. He's available now, but he won't be for long. It's important you make a decision quickly. If you want him, I'll need to know by the end of the weekend. If not, I'll place him with another family."

"Just like that?" I ask.

"Things can happen quickly."

"I was led to believe the process is excruciatingly slow."

"It is most of the time. As I said, your timing is perfect."

As it turns out, my timing is perfect, though it's hard to imagine how Jill can come to know such a thing in the span of a seven-minute conversation. Throughout my life I've always taken for granted that good things happen to me precisely because I'm in the right place at the right time. That, and I'm willing to commit. Good things happened when I met Rick and it feels like it is happening again when I see Sergey. I'm willing to push all my chips into the center of the table and draw the next card. I picture Jill as a tall woman who cares about her job, about finding homes for children she's never seen and by all accounts, may never lay eyes on. Children who will never understand how much a woman like Jill can influence their lives. "Before we celebrate," Jill says, "please take a look at the other documents I sent in the e-mail. There's a lot to read, so take your time. Oops. Scratch that. Read them tonight, and if you're still interested, call me in the morning and let me know."

"Is this normal?" I ask again.

"What do you mean?"

"How quickly do I have to decide? Like I said, most of what I've read indicated it can take one to two years."

"You called and he's available. It's that simple."

I scan the e-mail attachments—a ten-page introduction to the adoption agency, a thirteen-page contract, and a couple of pages on the Russian adoption process. I tell Jill I'll call her back tomorrow. I hang up and start reading. As I thumb through the paperwork, I find information regarding the costs. The Russian adoption will run us about 21,500 dollars. On page seven, I read about financing options, mainly through nonprofits that under the appropriate circumstances may be able to cover costs for those who need it. The information isn't so much practical as sales oriented, like whoever was assigned the chore of writing up the procedures felt I had to be talked into it. It feels like there is some subtle subtext behind the words, which makes me wonder: what am I not seeing?

The actual contract is exactly what you'd expect—pages of fine print putting most of the blame, if anything goes wrong, squarely on the adoptive parents. An hour later I've read all the information twice. Some of it three times. I call Rick at the hospital. It's way late. He sounds tired. "I've found our son," I say. Actually, I sort of shout it at him. I'm grinning ear-to-ear, giddy with adrenaline. "On the Internet. I think we've found our baby."

"Slow down," he says.

"I have two photos, no three if you count the girl, but I don't think we should count the girl. She's cute, that's not it. Not really, but I don't think she's for us. That leaves two pictures, one child."

"Slow down."

"His name's Sergey. Russian. In one, he's sitting and has this look I don't know how to explain other than he's perfect. He's, let's see, in the e-mail it says birthdate May, 19, 2006. He's 7.2 kg. What's that in pounds, I have no idea?"

"Honey, I'm at work," Rick says. "I have patients waiting on me."

"I just noticed it says head circumference 45 cm. Is that good? In the picture, he's all head, but I've no idea if 45 is good or what. Chest circumference 43 cm. This is three weeks ago. Wait, a month. A month ago his head was bigger around than his chest. Is that normal? Is there anyone there at the hospital you can ask?"

"Look, I'm excited for you."

"For us."

"Of course, for us. But I have one more patient to see."

"You work too hard," I say.

"We'll talk in a bit, I promise."

"One more thing."

"We'll talk."

"I'm reading the e-mail," I say. "I have test results right here in front of me."

"What kind of tests."

"HIV negative. Syphilis negative. Hepatitis negative. TB negative. That's all good, right?"

"Where did this information come from? How do we know it's accurate?"

"There's more. You'll like this; it says Dr. Cardiologist- healthy. EKG—normal. Ultrasound of organs—normal. Endocrinologist—healthy."

"This is an adoption agency we're talking about, right?" Rick says. "Not some crazy Russian posting kids for sale. This isn't Craig's List."

"I found a woman, Jill something, out of Illinois, north somewhere. Near Chicago, I think. We spoke on the phone. She says we have to move fast. We have this evening to think about it."

"And?"

"If we want him, we have to express mail 3,000 dollars on Monday."

"Monday's Memorial Day."

"I mean Tuesday. First thing."

"So we have an extra day to think it over."

"To think what over?"

I hear Rick breathing on the other end of the phone, probably silently counting to ten before he answers. "We'll talk when I get home," he says. He speaks in a low voice, the words enunciated clearly so there's no confusion. "Give me an hour and I'll see you then."

"This is the right thing to do," I half shout at him. "I feel it. I want to do this."

"Okay, okay. Let's talk when I get home."

I press the phone to my ear. "I'll go down to the bank first thing Tuesday and grab a cashier's check."

"We'll talk." He hangs up.

I stare at the image of Sergey on my laptop. His eyes are blue, his face pink, and I can see the hint of tiny veins zigzagging across his fuzzy head. I know he is ours, I know it, I feel it. I am in love. If we don't take him, someone else will. He'll be gone, our baby will be gone. Jill said that's the way it works. We have to move quickly.

By the time Rick pulls into the drive, I've read all the paper work a half dozen times and it's a done deal. My mind's made up about Sergey. The only question is do we want another child and if so, boy or girl? Rick's not talking. He's listening. He shakes his head and says we want two boys. "They could be perfect playmates," he said.

On Monday morning, Jill sends photos of two more Russian baby boys and all the health stats for both. The first child is Stanislav, a boy the report describes as "left at the orphanage two months after birth." The second is Dmitry, born on September 20, 2005 and "given up at infancy." The story with Dmitry is that he was scheduled to go to another family, but something went haywire and it didn't happen. I read that he's had several colds, bronchitis, and chicken pox. He's also had a hernia that has since been corrected. Dmitry's apparently not in perfect health, but when Rick and I take a look at the photos, we want him, no question about it. There is something about his defiant but vulnerable expression. He needs us and we need him.

I e-mail Jill our decision—we want Sergey *and* Dmitry. Can do, she says and reminds me again to move quickly or risk losing the boys. Our task is to fill out the paperwork, sign the contract, and send money. It sounds easy enough, yet the contract itself takes some time to read and hours to complete. We have to list family names, addresses, places of birth, passport numbers, employers, positions, income, social security numbers, and a long list of other information. By the time I've filled in the blanks, my fingers are stiff and my wrist hurts. We put the cashier's check and the contract into an envelope and that envelope into a larger express mail envelope and off it goes.

Tuesday morning, I call Jill. "It's on its way," I say. My voice is enthusiastic to the point of sounding squeaky.

"This is only the beginning," she says.

"I understand," I say, though in truth I don't.

"It's important you begin putting together your dossier. Get it to me as soon as you can and I'll submit it to the Russian Department of Education."

Our dossier is a spectacularly long list of certifications and notarized documents that Rick and I must track down. It includes birth certificates, marriage license, letters of reference, letters of employment, financial statements, tax returns, and copies of real estate deeds. It includes prickly medical exams—blood work, a listing of diseases found or not found, many of which we've never heard of. This includes neurological disorders, substance abuse, cancer, disabling trauma, "disorder of internal organs" and "disorder of locomotor apparatus," among others. (I'd like to believe my "locomotor apparatus" was working or I'd be painfully aware it wasn't). Our dossier includes a police clearance from the Department of Justice on Delaware State letterhead, post placement registration obligation affidavits, parent questionnaires, copies of passports, and other documents way too numerous and boring to list here.

"What comes after the dossier?" I ask Jill.

"Once it's approved, you need to be ready to travel. New York to Moscow and on to Novokuznetsk. The whole trip will take five days, seven max."

"How much notice will we receive?"

"It depends," she says.

"On what?"

"I've no idea. It's best just to be ready."

"Then I get to see my babies?"

"Let's take it one step at a time."

To a normal person, the speed we're moving seems shady at best. Here's the thing: I believe her. This isn't some sort of adoption sales pitch, I'm almost certain of it. It feels right, like one of those moments in life when the stars align and dreams come true. That's what I tell myself: this is a dream come true. Rick isn't so sure, but keeps quiet. He wants proof. He wants guarantees.

Call me gullible if you like, but I possess something Rick doesn't. Unbridled confidence. I'd spent hours, days, whole weeks sometimes, surfing the Internet reading everything I could on the adoption process—the pitfalls, the hassles, the disenchantment. I know all about the potential for disappointment, but I'm smitten to jibbers with the boys and I'm more than willing to risk significant cash if there's a chance of putting my arms around these two. I've done just what adoptive parents warn you not to do: I've fallen in love with the photos. As for the cost, I understand it's a lot of money. I also know we'd already blown a mountain of it on three failed IVF procedures.

About the time Jill is tearing though the envelope containing our first check, she calls and says she needs the dossiers.

"You're sure this is going to work?" I ask.

"You mean can I promise you Sergey and Dmitry? The answer is no, I can't." I know by now, Jill doesn't sugarcoat. Once your dossiers are approved, I'll need another check. No later than fifteen days before you travel. It's all there in the contract. You probably don't want to hear this, but you need to trust me."

"I trust you," I tell her. "I do."

Rick is a little queasy about the situation and naturally has a simple solution. Prior to finding Sergey and Dmitry, we already had planned a trip to Napa Valley for the end of June for a little wine tasting tour. As luck would have it, the agency has a small secondary office in northern California and Rick suggests we swing by and make sure the whole thing isn't a mirage. The offices are located in Lafayette, California, about an hour south of Napa. I politely explain the idea to Jill. "Good move," she says.

The agency's Lafayette office is hidden away in the middle of a vast industrial park not far from San Francisco. After a few wrong turns in the rental car with no navigation system, we find the office and knock on the door. No one answers so I crack the unlocked door and yoo-hoo for whoever might be inside. The place is just what you'd expect only more so. Drab walls, metal furniture, a desk and chair with no one sitting there patiently, waiting for adoption-crazed parents to wander in. The walls are a beige color that looks either poorly painted or slightly dirty, I can't tell which. On top of the dull walls someone has plastered hundreds of faces of babies. Round, smooth and grinning mugs staring back at us. All the poses ooze simple pleas. Help. I need parents. I'll be a good kid, I promise.

From where I stand, I can see down a hallway and through a sliver of doorway. I spot two women, both with shoulders slumped over piles of file folders on their respective desks. One of the women looks up, sees me eyeing her, and hurries out to greet us. This is Ally. We shake hands and she calls for the other women, Cheryl. We all stand there staring at each other when Rick says, "Why don't you let us take you two to lunch?"

Rick is ready to move things along.

Ally and Cheryl choose an Italian restaurant a couple of blocks from the office. Lunch is a way for Rick and I to see what these two are *really* like, if they are the type to take all our money and zoom off to

Cuernavaca when we turn our backs. Turns out both women love their jobs. Both adore babies. Both feel a deep-seated urge to right injustices and international adoptions is just the challenge to keep their juices flowing. I grumble about all the paper work and Ally's face goes slack. She too is a paper hater. Then she switches the conversation to babies and her expression blossoms. She's placed babies from Russia, Kazakhstan, Nepal, Bulgaria, Uganda, and a bunch of hardscrabble countries. I'm halfway through a Caesar salad when I decide she's legit and a genuinely nice person. She wants nothing more than to save babies from growing up parentless. And she cares about the parents, about Rick and me, that we understand what we're getting into, that we are committed enough to carry this thing out.

"It's tough," she says. "The process. It can test you in ways you haven't been tested."

"How so?" I ask.

"When you see the babies for the first time, emotions can run high. You never know what'll happen."

"The parents' emotions, you mean?"

"The children. They don't know you. They can be frightened, aggressive, resentful, shy. Who knows? Some just aren't in the mood to meet anyone new." Ally takes a messy bite of her fettuccini Alfredo. "Be prepared for the worst. A lot of these kids have problems. Some multiple problems. It can be the reason Russian families don't want them."

"What kinds of problems?" Rick asks.

"Russian babies are born smaller and sicker than in years past and those are the lucky ones. Ten percent don't make it to term. Poverty, drugs, alcohol, it all takes a toll." Ally cocks her head at me, her pretty face flicking up at me. Cheryl is about to say something but decides not to. "Look," Ally says, "I know this is bad news, but it's important you go into this with your eyes open."

"But Dmitry and Sergey are healthy," I say.

"The paperwork says they're basically healthy. It always says they're healthy."

"Are you suggesting they're not?" I ask.

"I'm not sure what I'm suggesting."

This isn't what I want to hear. I want reassurances. I want someone to tell me that my children have beaten the odds. I'm dreaming, but I want it in writing. I peek at Rick, a man suddenly mesmerized by his grilled shrimp caprese. He pushes a forkful of angel hair round the rim of a giant yellow-ochre dish keeping his head down and eyes firmly on a little ball of melted mozzarella. This is his way of saying "It's up to me." This whole thing was my idea. The baby, the IVF, the adoption. I'm the driving force behind the antics of the last year or so. Rick is happy as berry sorbet to live the life we have. He's overjoyed with just the two of us. And I've no room to argue. I love what we have. I just want more.

From nowhere Ally says, "I think now is the perfect time to tell you your dossiers were approved." I just got word before you arrived." She lifts her glass of diet Dr. Pepper. "I think a toast is in order." We all raise our glasses. "To a safe trip," she says.

Rick finally looks up. I put my ice water down delicately on the tabletop.

Ally says, "If you want to make this happen, you two need to be on a flight to Russia within a week. Sooner if you can make it."

Ally suggests we get a move on because there's much to do. First, we have the issue of visas for Rick and I. We immediately leave the offices and head to San Francisco to start our visa paperwork. Without the visas the nice people at JFK International Airport won't let us get near the plane. Ally rattles off a list of visa agencies—Downtown Travel, Russian Connections, International Adoption Travel—all of which I scribble on a napkin. Her voice is rushed, breathless, projecting just a hint of hopelessness, as if we're already too late. "Any of the agencies I just gave you," she says, "they can do what we need, pronto."

Second, we have to squeeze in a somewhat rushed Napa getaway where Rick and I sip wines all up and down St. Helena Highway, the main drag through the town, and get our fill of some spectacular vino—a crisp Cakebread chardonnay, a flamboyant Schrader T6 cabernet sauvignon, and a raspberryish Los Carneros pinot noir, to name those I can remember before my memory goes fuzzy.

And third, we need airline tickets to Moscow with a connecting flight to Novokuznetsk. All of this is last minute, of course, and I moan just thinking about the price of the tickets. Oh, I almost forget item number four. Before leaving the agency's office, it's time to write another check.

After Napa, we fly home to Delaware. The visas arrive soon thereafter. With the visas in hand, I get on the internet and connect to Aeroflot, the largest airline in Russia.

I finally get the tickets booked a whopping twenty-three hours ahead of our departure time. Rick has his own chores to tend to. He begins rescheduling his patients. He doesn't tell them he's heading off to Russia where he and his wife hope to eventually return with two healthy baby boys. I don't know what he tells them, but it works because he manages to keep them at bay long enough to spend six apprehensive days in a country known for its vodka, the Russian mafia, and a scowling Vladimir Putin.

To his partner doctors and nurses, Rick serves up the truth: that at fifty-one he's adopting a couple of Russian tykes. The fifty-one part they already know. The adopting part comes as a surprise. A shocker, really. To hear Rick tell it, both the doctors and nurses politely tell him he's nuts. "What the hell?" they say with nowhere to take the conversation. Then they tell him, "Well, go on, and go if you're going. We'll cover for you until you return."

So we do.

On July 2, 2007, only three days after returning from California, we're off to John F. Kennedy International Airport where we check in at international departures, hand over our passports and visas, receive a nod and a practiced smile from a moderately foreign-looking ticketing agent, a woman with round features and a bob hairdo straight out of the '60s, who probably looks great in a ushanka—a squarish Russian fur cap guaranteed to keep your ears from freezing off on cold nights trudging across an unforgiving Siberia—which is where we are headed.

Hunter first photo (Russia)

Dylan first picture (Russia)

Chapter Fourteen

Trip #1, Delaware to Novokuznetsk

O n the nine-hour flight to Moscow, I have oodles of time to pull out our itinerary and scan for anything I missed. Let's see. We are scheduled to land at Moscow's Sheremetyevo-2 airport in the morning, meet up with Oksana, our guide and translator, and get hustled off to our hotel. To locate your guide, do as follows: Exit plane, go through green light, stand in the center of the large terminal room, look for a sign that says Bbixoahn or something close, turn to your left and spot a café called Hleb & Sol (translated bread and salt) and there she'll be, Oksana, looking sprite and cheery sipping a mud-thick café con leche.

Rick and I march off the plane and immediately deviate from the plan by veering into the nearest bathrooms. I need to rejigger my money belt. It's strapped around my waist with $10,000 in cash neatly sealed inside. Rick is sporting his own money belt with another ten thou. Between us we were toting a pile of undeclared money through airports, across the Atlantic, and now into a formerly communist country led by underpaid bureaucrats who for all I know might frisk us, grab the dough, and sentence us to life in prison all in a Moscow minute. Our instructions are clear. Wrap the cash tightly, all new $100 bills, no marks, tears, dirt marks, creases, folds, rips, or any other markings. Plan ahead, our instruction sheet says. We were told we may have to go to several banks to find bills in such condition, but believe it or not, I had pre-ordered our crisp 100's from our local bank. Three lines down, the instruction sheet more or less order us to keep our yap shut about the money, which naturally squelches any possibility of asking why the greenbacks have to appear so freshly minted. At lunch, I recall Ally saying, "Don't ever discuss money with anybody you meet."

"Like who?"

"Like anyone."

"No, really, who can't we tell?" I ask.

"Really," she says. "You can't tell anyone."

Russian customs regulations limit undeclared cash to $10,000 per person, so in a way, we could make a case for squeezing in under the wire. If that were true, then we aren't technically breaking any laws. Only it's not true. In addition to the freshly minted baby cash we have spending money. Cash-wise we *are* breaking the law, but only by a bit, if that matters.

I nudge my way around women and luggage to a surprisingly clean stainless steel sink, lean forward and squint at myself in the mirror. My face is a tad puffy and my feet hurt, but all in all I look nothing like a lawbreaker. If the lack of guilt were a measure of criminal prowess, I'd get an F. I don't show it, but I'm scared stiff I'll get tripped up by some money-sniffing Russian hound who can smell crisp one hundreds a kilometer away. Even if Rick and I do make it out of the airport with the dough, there are the Russian taxi drivers to deal with. These are guys, so I've been assured on the Internet, who look sweet as vanilla ice cream and who then cart unsavvy foreigners like us into the countryside, shoot us, and take our wallets (or our not-so-hidden money belts).

We meet up outside the bathrooms. Rick eyes my waist trying to spot any tale tail sign of the money. "Is everything okay?" he asks.

"I'm itchy and sweaty," I say and reach through my shirt for the money belt and push it down on my waist.

"Don't do that," he says and frowns at me, doing his best to look not guilty.

"Who's going to see? These people?" I wave at travelers inches from my hand rushing off to who knows where.

"So we're ready?" he says.

"I'm hungry. I'm tired." I scrunch up my nose. "I think the big guy next to me on the plane sweat on me. I stink."

Rick glances over my head. "I don't see a green light."

"Honey, did you hear me?"

"You smell fine," he says and looks straight at me. "Really," he says and my husband has a way of using the simplest words and gestures to get his message across.

I half-turn and take a casual, calculated look back the way we came and then the other way where the terminal opens up into a large room.

"Are you ready to do this?" he says.

This? And I wonder what he means, but I give the money belt another tug where the Velcro is digging into my waist and say, "Yes, I am."

We begin our search for the illusive green light, follow the trail, and surprisingly find Oksana just where she's supposed to be. The woman is all teeth and smile. She's youngish, fair hair and skin and reminds me of a college freshman, one of those not entirely sure of herself or where she fits in. She has a cup of something hot in one hand and a small white sign in the other with the word "SIMONS" written in blocky, semi-Russian-looking lettering.

Oksana quickly ushers us outside to a car with a driver who she promises won't murder us. From terminal to car takes seconds, and I get the feeling the trick to avoiding unseen danger is to keep moving. Oksana sits without bothering to fasten her seatbelt. In Russian, she tells the driver to get a move on. He says something that I take to mean "Where to?" and I hear the words "Ritz Carlton" come out of Oksana's mouth clear as a bell. On the way, the driver is proud to tell us that Moscow has recently, for the second year in a row, earned the dubious award of world's most expensive city. "Is great honor," he says.

"I thought New York or maybe Tokyo held that honor," Rick says.

"No, no. On this, I am sure. My beloved Moscow is winner."

All I see of the driver is a mostly bald head and the back of a dirty shirt collar. The edges of the collar are worn bare.

"How can people afford to live here?" Rick asks.

"You are right. The people, they cannot afford."

"I see," Rick says and smiles, but it's not a real smile, no wrinkles at the edges of the eyes. This is one of those polite this-is-going-nowhere smiles and means he'll stop talking.

"It's a beautiful city," I say always the one to put an encouraging spin on things. In truth, it's too early for appraisals. That, and we're an hour north of Moscow anyway. I'm bone tired from the flight and what little I can see of the drive is far from beautiful. What I see outside my smudged window is a dark gray highway, gray concrete buildings, and a gray sky overhead. It looks an awful lot like the dumpier sections of New Jersey. And it's hot, my guess is 80, 90 degrees and a humidity hovering around 100 percent, though it's not raining.

"The drive," I ask, "how long will it take?" I know the answer. I'm just making conversation.

The driver makes a spitting sound with his lips, or maybe he actually spits on the steering wheel, and says, "Twenty minutes, two hours, who can know such a thing."

I turn and stare out the window into the glare. "It's a nice drive, nonetheless."

"Yegor," the man says and it comes out as E-gore, heavy on the E.

"I'm Sharon," I say to the back of the mostly bald head. "This is my husband, Rick."

Yegor glances up into the mirror and squints at me, or winks, or possibly he's eyeing the car behind us riding our dented bumper.

As for the high prices, Yegor is right, of course. In scheduling the hotel, I managed to save us a bundle on the room using American Express. Even with the discount, the suite at the Ritz comes to almost $500 a night. With my tired feet, sore back, and sweat trickling down the inside of my shirt and a money belt giving me worry hives, it's worth every cent.

"The Ritz," Yegor says sometime later, "is in heart of city. Close to Kremlin," he says and I can't tell if this is a joke or I'm supposed to coo. "The Bolshoi Theatre," Yegor says, "and Grand Conservatory Hall." He points out other sights I've never heard of and can't pronounce.

We near downtown and the traffic slows. We cruise up Tverskaya Street, pass Red Square, and pull under the ornate truss-like structure of the Ritz Carlton entrance. The façade is lit up like a night scene in a thriller movie set in Europe, even though it's well before noon. The place has a tingly restrained presence, eleven stories and three hundred or so of the largest rooms in the city, so my guidebook says. The entranceway and the parking area are filled with Mercedes and BMWs, a few newer Audis. Rick pays Yegor what looks like several hundred rubles and shakes his hand, which Yegor isn't expecting, and we get hustled inside the hotel lobby by no less than five bellmen. We register and are scooted along to our room with an efficiency that would shame New York's Waldorf Astoria. Our suite has wood moldings, heated marble floors in the bathrooms, and a control panel by the bed to run the curtains back and forth without expending any extra effort.

I yank off my money belt and hide it in a draw under a vintage J.Crew sweater I'm sure no one would suspect was covering ten grand in shiny new bills, and suddenly, I'm fresh as a meadow violet. Just ridding myself of that thing has boosted my mood and given me a shot of energy. After we unpack, Rick and I decide to go downstairs and see if we can make the trek to Red Square without getting jacked for what's left in our wallets. The Square is exactly two hundred meters that-a-way, the concierge tells us as he points a manicured finger out of the Ritz's massive front doors. We find the Square a block away and it's anything but square. In fact, there isn't a right angle in the place. Lenin's Mausoleum, the domed Saint Basil's Cathedral, the Kremlin, and the State Historic Museum— the architecture is breathtaking. There is also a luxury shopping mall featuring Gucci, Louis Vuitton, Burberry, and Prada, to name a few. The opulence of the designer stores is a bit overwhelming, and for a country struggling seems oddly out of place.

We walk around the square observing and I begin to think about my two baby boys. This is their country, their culture, and I should definitely learn all I can. I wonder if they have a connection, at such young ages, to their homeland. Will they ever want to return? Rick and I discuss naming them and decide to keep their Russian names as middle names. I visualize their tiny faces and fantasize about them growing up to be strong young men. We are so close to seeing them and I can't wait to hold them. My anticipation is growing by the hour and not even the strolling and window shopping calms me. Perhaps a good meal of authentic Russian cuisine will help.

Back at the hotel we ask the concierge for dinner suggestions and he recommends the Caviarterra. "The menu is Russian. Some Georgian, but you will like it."

"It's Georgian, but I'll like it?" I ask.

"Oh, yes. Caviar, borsch, chicken Kiev, anything you want."

"Stroganoff?"

"You've eaten the stroganoff?"

"An American version. I'm sure it's not the same."

"A friend, she tells me the schi is delicious." When I shrug, as if to say I've never heard of schi, she says, "Is a soup made from sauerkraut. Not so popular as borsch, but the color is better."

What the heck? We're in Moscow, so we give the place a try.

The Caviarterra restaurant is in fact as advertised, dark and ornate, like something out of a fifty-year old Russian movie. When our waiter arrives, Rick orders us two glasses of French wine, a Rhône for me and a Bourgogne Cote de Beaune for him. We listen to the specials—whole baked starlet, spicy stewed veal, a traditional wiener schnitzel—all of which sound glorious, chiefly because I haven't eaten anything solid since somewhere over the Atlantic hours earlier.

For dinner, I order the beef fillet with pommes frites and Rick orders pike perch with a horseradish crust. As promised, the food is delicious. We throw caution to the wind regarding Moscow prices and order another glass of wine each. We return to our room full, relaxed, and ready for bed. Tomorrow will bring us even closer to our boys.

Oksana stands near the hotel entrance, looking sun-starved and cheery as ever. She waves, says her good mornings, and asks about our sleep. She does all this while rushing us out the door to a waiting car. The car, a Lada 110, is old and dented, nothing like the glistening sedans parked neatly under the hotel's porte cochere. Our chariot is the color of overripe cucumber with accents of rust. We crawl in and get comfortable.

Yegor is behind the wheel wearing the same shirt as yesterday. He revs the engine until it's screaming like a maimed cat. Other hotel guests stop and stare. He lets the whine die down, then presses on the pedal a couple of more times. When he's good and ready we zoom away into the big city of Moscow.

We take Tverskaya Street to Leningrad Avenue and veer onto the M-10 heading sort of north and west out of the city. I know this because every mile or so I see a giant blue and white sign reading M-10. I keep track of our route because I'm secretly afraid of getting lost, of being stranded in a strange land with no breadcrumbs to follow home.

If you look at a map of Moscow you'd discover that the highway system looks much like a dartboard with the Ritz and Red Square forming the bull's-eye. The city is surrounded by three rings, (three highways), and as we scoot out of downtown and pass each ring the glitzy metropolis as I've come to know it fades away. The buildings along the highway turn muted and drab, the colors muddy. I see an occasional twenty-story clay box that I take to be housing blocks where people live out modest and presumably unfulfilled lives. The outer city has a grizzled industrial feel to it. The only color, a dreary yellow-ochre, comes from the electric trolleys that criss-cross the city. Adding to the mechanized feel, the trolley lines bring with them a ridiculous infrastructure of messy electrical cables suspended over the streets that remind me of strands of hair on a bad-hair day. Mostly I gaze out my own window, occasionally looking past my calm husband to see what's on the other side. Up ahead I see a string of low billboards on the median advertising vodka and expensive cars.

Every fifteen minutes or so the traffic slows to a snarl of cars. All I see in front of us are break lights and bumpers. The disheartening view from the back seat notwithstanding, the drive couldn't be worse. Harrowing, really.

Yegor is the worst driver in this world or any other.

He drives fast. Too fast, if you want to live. He breaks too hard and too often. He jerks the wheel left and right and left and right tossing us around like bobble-head characters on a rickety rollercoaster. He edges along side of a car ready to pass and then (well before he actually passes the car) swerves into the other car's lane triumphantly claiming his territory. To make matters worse other drivers do the same like this is all a game of nerves at high speed.

We arrive at the Sheremetyevo International Airport slightly panicked. To be fair, Yegor is far from panicked; rather, he's downright proud of his performance and revs the engine as Rick pulls our bags from the trunk. It's Oksana, Rick and I who are agitated partly because of the drive and partly because we're late. Oksana hurries us to the ticketing agent, who moves in slow motion, and on to the security station closest to our terminal where she dumps us and where we get shouted at, wanded, glared at, and frisked by airport security.

Yesterday we flew into town on a somewhat worn Boeing 767. Today we are zipping across country in what looks like a broken-down flying Greyhound bus. I hurry on board with my wheeled carry-on. The aisles are narrow and I bump knees and bang elbows with grumpy travelers too stubborn to scoot over. I collide with an older gentleman who grunts at me in Russian, or possibly Belarusian, and he raises a hand as if to slap me or wave me away. The whole incident takes about a millisecond, but the feeling of vulnerability lingers with me for the rest of the flight. One small misstep, one slight or disrespectful word, or a stupid bump on the knee with a roller carry-on can change everything and the last thing I want is for everything to change. I want things to go just as planned. I want everyone to get along. I want the orphanage to locate good parents (Rick and me). I want good parents (ditto) to find loving, healthy sons with clear eyes and strong bodies ready to hop into our arms the moment they spot us. Right now, I want our rattlebag of a plane to arrive in Novokuznetsk without an airborne collision, a midair explosion, or forced landing on some backwoods Siberian river. Rick is up ahead of me and locates our seats. He wrestles into the window seat and looks up at me and then at my offending roller bag, which seems to have grown larger in proportion to the skimpy seats. "Put it in the overhead," he says.

"There is no overhead," I half shout at him.

Rick shoves his soft bag under the seat in front of him. "Here, hand it to me."

I heave my carry-on into his lap and sit beside him. "Now what?"

"It's fine where it is. You just settle in."

"Give it to me." I grab the bag and proceed to jam it between my legs onto the floor, where it rests, not even close to fitting under the seat. I put my feet on top of the bag, my knees in the air in an attractive posture much like giving birth.

The motor of the jets kicks in. The noise is loud and mechanical, like a car with a bad starter.

Rick leans over and half whispers, half shouts in my ear. "Remember why we're here."

"I remember," I say.

"We're here to see our boys."

"I remember."

"We're here to start a family," Rick says.

"I remember already."

I'm in a mood and Rick is trying to make it better, but I'm a-okay where I am, bad mood and all. Deep down, I'm wondering if I need this, that I'm supposed to learn a thing or two about tolerance, hardship and risk. Rick would say I'm overreacting. He'd tell me to stay centered, not to get distracted by the little stuff. He'd tell me he loves me and everything's going to be all right, and he'd say it like he believed it, (he would believe it), and I'd believe it too. I lean my knees over and lay them on Rick's lap.

A split second after our rubbery tires leave the ground the guy behind me lights up a cheap Russian cigarette and blows smoke in my hair. Soon other passengers light up and the entire cabin smells like burning gym shoes. I glare at Rick who shrugs and blinks at me, the blinking shorthand for "I love you. It'll be all right." I close my eyes and take shallow breaths in hopes of avoiding the onset of lung cancer and try to get some shut-eye.

Fat chance. Thirty minutes into the flight the entertainment begins—an honest to goodness fistfight—but we can't see the actual event from the cheap seats. Thick-bottomed flight attendants break it up and send the fighters back to their corners, where everyone cools down and no one bothers to come out for a second round.

Seven hours.

That's how long I squirm in my seat trying to find a comfortable position for my raised knees. In all that time, I don't find it.

We land at Novokuznetsk Airport where we use the bathroom, rejigger our money belts, and stand around craning our necks looking for our guide. She's a no-show. We have little choice but to put on that dopey, universal expression common to lost tourists. I stare at approaching travelers hoping they will offer an encouraging word. Nothing. We don't have a car. We don't know our way around, our hotel name or where exactly it is located. And even if we were in possession of A and B above, we don't know where the baby house is (a big secret, it turns out), and thus can't do what we came to do without our guide. I spot a group of smiling Midwesterners who departed our plane and who are in Siberia for the sole purpose of running a church camp for poor Siberian kids. Maybe they'll take pity on us and offer to help. I spot a woman in the group who looks in charge and I approach her.

I spell out our predicament.

We chat for a few moments, weighing several ideas: piling in with the church-goers who don't really have the room but nonetheless agree to drop us in town, calling for a taxi, or standing our ground and praying that our absent guide and driver magically appear sometime before dark. Their leader, Kathleen, hands me a piece of paper with a telephone number written in tiny script. She says, "Listen, if things go bad, call me."

The Midwesterners adios and an hour later our guide, Natasha, comes running at us apologizing from forty feet away in a mixture of Russian and English. The reason she's late is apparently complicated. I smile and take deep breaths, silently thanking God, as if Rick and I had survived some traumatic hardship and near-fatal experience, when in fact the delay was only mildly irksome.

We are introduced to a beat-up minivan and a new driver who doesn't offer his name, but grunts a hello.

The driving in Moscow was bad, yet out here in the hinterlands, in the real Russia, where even now you can sense how bleak life must have been under the hammer and sickle, the driving is worse. Twenty minutes into our jaunt into town, we come upon a fresh wreck. I know this because steam is rising from the smashed front end of one car, the rear of the other car equally crumpled, and both cars sit there immovable in the middle of the road. Both drivers, men with no necks and large stomachs, stand in the highway scratching their chins, as if to say, "How did this happen?"

Vehicles swerve around the jumble of glass and metal parts doing seventy or better as calmly as can be. Nobody slows, including us, but makes a split-second decision to cut left or right at the last moment and swing into an adjoining lane without so much as a blinker or a sideways glance.

"Is it always like this?" I ask Natasha.

"No, no. Is not usually so hot this time of year."

"I mean the traffic, the accidents. I don't see anyone staying in their own lane."

Our driver says, "When someone comes at you, is important not to show fear. Is easy. If you like, I can teach you."

To show his driving prowess, he jams his foot on the accelerator and we speed up until our poor minivan is shaking and clacking like an old train, then he swerves out into oncoming traffic with the intention of passing an equally beat-up minivan weighed down with a dozen passengers. Up ahead in the distance, I can see a car coming at us. Rather than slow and pull back into our lane, our driver, who I now think of as Yegor 2, puts all his considerable weight onto the pedal and presses it into the floorboard. For long excruciating seconds, we approach the oncoming car while the driver coming at us. None of us are seat-belted (because there are no seatbelts), though at this speed and driving a decade old tin can it probably doesn't matter.

I reach for Rick's hand and dig my fingernails into his palm.

With what feels like a inches to spare, the van on our right nudges over, the oncoming car eases to his right, and a gap appears just wide enough to squeeze a narrow-bodied Russian-made minivan through at seventy miles an hour. The oncoming car goes whizzing by, the driver on our right looks over and winks, and Yegor 2 leans forward and wipes some grime from the windshield with his fingers and sets his sights on the road ahead. I release my grip on my husband's hand, take a breath, and resume staring out the window counting the seconds until I can escape from this heap.

By the time we arrive at the hotel, my heart rate is almost back to normal.

The front of the hotel is lit by several small dim lights and I can see that it looks as beat up as our minivan but with more years on it. Natasha and Yegor 2 say their so-longs as Rick and I stand with bags in hand knocking on the front door of the hotel. The door is locked and the entire place looks shut down for the night. I knock and knock. My knuckles are raw by the time a slightly aggravated woman appears and opens up, hands us a key, points up the stairs, shows us three gnarled fingers (meaning, I assume, that our room is on the third floor), and never once asks our names.

"Carry me," I say to Rick.

"Give me your bag," he says.

"No. I mean it. I'm exhausted."

Rick puts our bags on the floor and flexes his neck. "I will if you need me to," which is all I need to hear to know that my husband loves me. I grab hold of my carry-on and trudge up three flights to a room the length and width of a medium-sized walk-in closet. It's dank with the slightly awful smell of rotting wood, carpet, or small animal, something organic and decomposing in any event. The room has two twin beds on opposite sides of the room. A bathroom but no shower. No thermostat. No air conditioning. No screens on the windows.

"It must be 1,000 degrees in here," I say.

Rick drops his travel bag and sinks into one of the beds. "I may have heat stroke."

"Before you go unconscious, can you open a window?" I ask, and when he does a cloud of hateful Siberian mosquitoes rush at us as if they'd been knocking for some time.

I unzip my bag and pull out a fresh can of bug spray. "Do me," I say. "What?"

"Spray my arms, right here. Spray everything, I don't care."

Our instructions said to bring mosquito nets and bug repellent. We opted to ignore the nets (they couldn't possibly mean it) and instead snagged a can of Off. We spray each other. Then we spray the beds and walls and floors and double-coat the window sash and sill. It doesn't make any difference. Angry skeeters see us as dinner and don't let up until we undress and hide under the covers. Novokuznetsk is so far north the sun almost never sets in summer, or at least it feels that way. Even under the heavy-duty sheet it's as light as an operating room, 10,000 degrees with the window wide open, and the mosquitoes are making more noise than a construction crew.

"Turn out the light," I say from under the sheet.

"It is out."

"How about we close the drapes?"

"And what, suffocate in our sleep."

"Yeah, I think that's what I mean."

"Remember why we're here," he says.

"I remember."

Chapter Fifteen

Envelope No. 2
·····································

I manage to get ten minutes of shut-eye just about the time the entire town of Novokuznetsk breaks into a monster of a party. Outside our window I hear horns honking and people shouting. It has the ruckus feel of a New Orleans-style celebration that never ends. We learn later that the Olympic Committee just announced that Russia had been selected to host the 2014 XXII Olympic Winter Games. Good news for Russia, bad news for two tired Americans here to start a family.

In the morning we head down to the hotel restaurant. A woman with muscled arms I swear I'd seen minutes ago hustling in and out of rooms on the third floor carrying linens arrives at our table and asks if we'd like breakfast. Our responses are restricted to *da* or *nyet*. In no time two plates of food show up, each with one overly fried egg, a tepid pink hot dog, and a lump of graying mayonnaise.

Our hotel appears to be a home base for several American adoption agencies working with local orphanages. The small breakfast room is filled with Americans, most sporting confused, lost expressions and all here to visit various orphanages in hopes find their future children. A man at the next table leans back in his chair and stares at Rick. "It's not what I thought," he says. "I do everything they tell me and not a damn thing is as it should be."

"My wife and I just arrived," Rick says. "Any advice?"

"Don't believe any of it," he says.

A woman sitting across from him says, "Walter, don't start."

"You've had a rough time of it," Rick says.

Walter is big-headed and big-eared. He's wearing one of those plaid lumberjack shirts. "The airport they have in Moscow, Shere-whatever, it was a madhouse. We practically got mugged by the taxi drivers."

"I'm Nicki," the man's wife says to me. "One of the drivers, a kid really, grabbed hold of my arm and wouldn't let go. It was cute, in a way."

"It *was* chaotic," I say. "Did your agency arrange for a driver?"

"I had to give the kid a shove," Walter says. "Next time I enter the airport, I'm bringing a club."

"A driver?" Nicki says. "You had a driver?"

"And a guide."

"A guide?"

"To translate, take us to the hotel, pick us up the next day and make sure we made our flight here."

"No driver," Walter says. "Definitely no guide."

"What agency are you with?" Nicki asks.

I tell her and involuntarily reach for Rick's wrist, the one with the fork making tiny circles in the mayonnaise.

Walter says, "Are they as worthless as this bunch I'm with?"

"Not at all," I say. Suddenly, I feel the need to defend our agency. I don't mention the horrifying drives to and from airports or the flight from Moscow to Novokuznetsk. "I don't know what I expected," I say. "But in all, I don't think we have a complaint."

"When we arrived," Walter says to Rick, "we were just like you, all smiles and optimism. If fades, believe me."

Rick nods politely.

"Let's you and me talk in a couple of days," Walter says, "and you tell me if I'm wrong."

"When do you get to visit the orphanage?" I ask Nicki.

"Done deal," Walter says. He turns away from us glaring at the green walls. His lips move in small motions, carrying on an internal dialogue, his mouth opening then squeezing shut, the lips rounding into an O, and then he juts his jaw and bites down hard on a lower lip. He flinches as if feeling the pain.

"We've been," Nicki says. Her eyes go red and she begins to sob. "I hadn't planned for any of this."

Walter pushes the stumpy end of his hotdog around his plate. "The kid had, has, fetal alcohol syndrome. He was a mess. You ever see one of these kids? The face is flat as a pancake; the eyes are droopy like he's staring back at you through a rainy window. Only it's permanent."

"I'm familiar with the syndrome," Rick says.

"You hear about things like this, but to see it yourself rips you up inside."

"So what happens now?" I ask. "With you two, I mean."

"What happens?" Walter says, "I'll tell you what happens. I wouldn't touch that kid if he was the last homeless baby in Siberia. We told the lady there to keep him. I also gave the woman in charge, the director or whatever, an earful. You tell me why nobody told us about the baby's condition. You think they didn't know? You think someone forgot to mention, 'Mr. Guthrie, there's just one little item we overlooked: your adopted son's face is blank as a canvas. His muscle tone, well, he doesn't have any. Hope that's not a problem for you. As for what caused it, could be his mother downed a couple of bottles of cheap vodka every day for the last nine months, but we can't be sure.'"

"Walter, please," Nicki says.

"I have a right to state my case," he says.

"You're scaring these nice people."

"They ought to be scared."

Other people at other tables go quiet, listening.

"Walter, that's enough."

Walter leans nearer our table and half whispers, "I'm doing you folks a favor."

Nicki is pretty in a sharp-featured way. She pats Walter on the arm. "Walter here, he wanted a boy in the family. The adoption was his idea." He's clearly uncomfortable being talked about and if he were a mean man, which he's not, he'd bark at his wife to keep quiet. Instead, he squirms in his wooden chair and mashes at his eyes. "It was all so unexpected," she says, a look on her face as if she's still not entirely sure what happened. "We arrived happy to see our baby and then this. It was hard."

"They could have told us," Walter says.

"I know," Nicki says.

"They could have warned us."

"Would it have made a difference?" his wife says.

Walter stares at his wife and thinks about her question.

After breakfast Rick and I walk the streets for an hour, taking in the local scene and admiring the well-mannered people. On our way back to the hotel we run into another American couple, the Carters, and discover that Dave and Carole Carter are one of us: from the same agency. It turns out we'll be driving to the baby house together. The Carters have two adopted daughters at home in Colorado, both adopted in the U.S. This time around they opted for a boy from Russia. Carole speaks in crisp, short sentences. She is nervous about the unknown, about the process, the money and the absolute lack of guarantees.

We spend the afternoon meandering through town. Later the hotel manager suggests a couple of good restaurants for dinner and Rick invites the Carters to join us. The four of us walk to a nearby restaurant where the place has a storybook feel to it with dark woods and complicated textures on the walls and round-faced people hunkered around boxy tables guzzling vodka from small glasses one gulp at a time.

Dave Carter puts both hands on the table and leans forward. "I overheard part of the conversation this morning."

Carole tilts her head forward and sweeps the room glancing at people out of the corner of her eyes like a not so practiced American spy. "We've prepared ourselves," she says.

"For what?" I ask.

"Disappointment, I guess. It's not good to expect too much."

None of us really want to talk about the sad possibilities, the letdowns and disenchantment that may be awaiting us. Nonetheless, we delve into the imagined horrors of Russian orphanages, alcoholic mothers, poverty, joblessness, and other inspiring topics until we are all thoroughly depressed. Under the table, I squeeze Rick's leg just above the knee in an attempt to get him to squirm, laugh, spill his beer, or anything that will get us onto something more upbeat. That's when the singing begins. The restaurant is one of those all-in-one jobs—food, entertainment, social hub—and exactly what we need. Off in the corner a singer is belting out an American tune I can't remember the name of. The woman is rosy-skinned, full-lipped, and has a throaty voice that gets deeper each time she repeats the melody. We listen, clap, shout over the noise, and Rick and Dave order another beer and lean back in their chairs. If you didn't know any better, you'd think we were old friends right at home visiting our favorite haunt. We are enjoying ourselves, but the unspoken sentiment is that we are all passing the time until we meet our boys.

The following morning, Rick and I do as told: get up early and wait in the lobby. We meet the Carters there, all of us sleepy-eyed. Our guide and translator Natasha appears and ushers us to a waiting minivan. Behind the wheel sits the newest Yegor, number 3, an extremely large man with butterball hands and another wide neck. We settle in and Natasha, who smells delightful, says. "You have gifts?"

"All set," I say.

Our instructions included a detailed section on presents. We are *not* obligated to bring presents, the paper says, and then goes on for a page or more explaining who gets what, type, and price. As for number of gifts, we are expected (not obliged) to get a little something for two to four local Russian Adoption agency reps (two males and two females), three to five caregivers (usually all female), and something for a group of orphans at the baby house. If we do brings presents from overseas, we are not to bring several of the same kind because customs will tag us as profiteers and do something bad, though what is never stated.

"Okay, then," Natasha says. "We have one visit on the way."

"One visit?" I ask.

"Do not distress," she says and looks at me with droopy eyelids. "Will take only a few minutes. You will see."

Yegor 3 drives mercifully slow through town. He's in no apparent rush and once or twice evens glides the van to a stop. He turns up one side street after another, left and right, sometimes right and right and right, sometimes circling the block, or so it seems, in what I imagine is a maneuver designed to lose a trail (if this were a James Bond movie), or intended to disorient the four of us should we ever want to pinpoint the secret hideout of the baby house. We finally make it out of town. Yegor transforms into the kind of Russian driver I have grown to hate. He speeds up to around seventy mph zooming around curves where we all lean to our left and in my case squish my husband up against the door.

We glide by sagging homes made from logs and rough-cut lumber put together in long horizontal bands. The wood is dark and mostly unpainted. The homes have vertical windows and surrounding the windows are intricate wooden designs and hand-carved moldings, now weathered by a millennium of neglect. After minutes of staring, the houses all run together.

The minivan slows and we ease into a small village. Yegor 3 yanks us into a parking lot where we idle past a group of Soviet-style, cinderblock buildings, the region's version of low-income projects. The spare structures are slum-like and dilapidated, and in most parts of the world would have been condemned. We move at a crawl in front of an especially rumpled building while Yegor 3 stares intently out his side window. He rolls the window down and apparently sees what he's looking for, because he jams on the break and thrusts the gearshift into park and turns off the key in one not-so-fluid motion. Yegor rotates his head and stares at me. After a long pause, he grunts. My impression is the grunt is aimed all of us, but his chunky neck will only twist so far. This stop is a nuisance, the grunt says, and somehow my/our fault.

Natasha twirls around in her seat and faces the four of us. "Okay, you will give me the envelopes, please."

"Where are we?" I ask.

"Do not be concerned," she says. "Is not far."

"What's not far?"

"Where they show you the babies."

"I'm curious, is all."

Natasha glances at Yegor 3 and bites on her lower lip. "The envelopes, please," she says without looking at us. "The big one, not the small one."

I had forked over envelope number one in Moscow. This was envelope number two. Envelope number three is for later.

"You're not going to tell me are you?" I say.

Natasha stops biting her lip and glows at me, happy that I finally understand the way this works. I hand her a fat envelope from my purse (I'd given up on the money belt). She reaches for the Carters envelope, which I assume contains less since the Carters are adopting only one child, and she holds one envelope in each hand weighing the bundles of cash. She eyes me and then moves on to Carole, squinting at her, pausing for a while.

"Is perfect," Natasha says and hands the envelopes to Yegor 3 who doesn't bother to pocket the envelopes, but marches up to one of the buildings with two bulky envelopes dangling from his pudgy fingers. He stops in front of a gray door on the first floor, glances left and right, knocks, and takes two steps backward.

"Roll down the window," I say to Rick. "I can't see."

"Let's just sit tight," he says. It's the first thing he's said in a long time, and I generally take notice of firsts.

Carole murmurs "Why do I feel we might have been kidnapped and not know it?"

"Or worse," I say trying to be funny, but it's not funny. I was thinking of saying, "I'd rather not know," but this too is more sad than funny and best left unsaid.

Rick tilts his head a half-inch to his right and sighs, his way of saying let's hold it together here, and to me, the head/breathing combo means why not put a lid on the sarcasm. "What could be worse?" Carole asks, and I can tell by her voice she really wants to know. There is a hitch in her voice as if she's on the brink of a meltdown. "Where are we anyway?"

"Carole, honey," Dave says.

"Is not important," Natasha says. I want to reach up and give her a big pinch on the neck.

"Like, relative to the hotel?" Carole says.

"Everything's going to be fine," Dave says.

"Or that railroad station we passed some time ago?" she says. "Where is that from here?"

"Honey," Dave says and drags out the eeeee sound making sure she gets his point, which is, I suppose, that this isn't the greatest place to have a breakdown even if one is called for.

"See that tree? Is oldest tree in the motherland," Natasha says in a proud voice gesturing with her chin out the window.

"Guess how old."

"A hundred," I said.

"More than 2,000 years, this tree has been with us."

"I once read about a 2,000 year old Sequoia living in California," I feebly say. A long silence follows.

I take my eyes from Yegor and crane my head around taking in my surroundings. This is ridiculous, of course. I've no idea where we are. But I am fixated thinking about Yegor and this dubious, clandestine rendezvous we've been invited to without our express knowledge. And I worry about Carole who is nervous enough to wet herself if she doesn't get answers.

"We're lost," Carole sighs.

I give it three minutes before I see tears. "We're not lost," I say with utter conviction but don't in the slightest mean it.

"Then why do I feel lost?"

"You feel confused. In a few minutes we get to see our babies and the closer we get the more anxious and confused we get."

"How do you know what I feel?"

"Because I feel the same thing."

Rick reaches around me and gives my shoulder a hug. I can't tell if he's hugging me because he thinks I feel genuinely overwhelmed by my emotions or for my efforts to comfort Carole. "Look," Dave says, his face pointing at Yegor.

We all stare at Yegor's backside and the splintery wooden door in front of him now cracked open an inch. Someone peeks out, though I only catch the tip of a man's nose likely attached to a member of the Russian mafia. Whoever it is, he seems to confirm it's the trustworthy Yegor 3 bearing envelopes of cash. The door opens a full six inches. Yegor 3 says something, shakes his head and finally hands over the envelopes. He doesn't wait for a receipt, but trudges back to our minivan, jerks open the minivan door, and plops down hard in the seat.

After, we drive. And worry. And drive.

After another hour in the minivan we are spent. Carole is slumped in the far backseat, her head against the window whispering to herself. Dave stares forward, smiling at no one, his hand gently patting his wife's knee. I scan the countryside, taking it all in, hoping to remember details so someday I can relate this to the boys.

We slow and turn left down a road littered with potholes and come to a grouping of ugly multi-story buildings. Probably apartments. The surface of the buildings, unadorned boxes really, are covered in thousands of tiny grayish tiles, like those you might find in lining a bathroom shower, but here the look is more Russian grunge showcasing large cracks and wobbly patches of grout and cinderblock infill where windows used to be. If buildings could brood, these six or eight massive cement shoeboxes would be prime examples. From the upper windows, clothes hang over the sills (no balconies), some dripping water down the wall like tears. The trim at the corners of each dreary structure along with the metal stairs are painted a sad gray-blue. Think architecture stripped of all sense of art and human kindness and you'd have a good idea of where we were.

Yegor 3 says something in Russian.

Natasha says, "He says is baby house. There, on left side of car. That one."

"We're here?" I say.

"Is what you expected?" Natasha asks.

I look at Rick, but he won't meet my eyes. He's glaring at the baby house.

Chapter Sixteen

The Baby House, Again

We exit the car, our group including Natasha wearing her glasses and a ball cap, the Carters, Carole still wobbly from the drive, and ourselves. Yegor stays with vehicle and lights up a cigarette. No babies in sight.

We enter the baby house and stand just inside the door, adjusting to the pervasive glumness of the place as if it were a darkened room and we needed the time to let our eyes do whatever eyes do to see in the dark. Carole and Dave Carter are as anxious as we are.

The ladies who work here know we are coming and immediately a wide-bodied woman clomps our way carrying a blond-haired baby boy. The boy is dressed in adorable blue-checkered overalls, white socks, and blizzard blue shoes that I can tell from here have never been worn. I can also tell that he's not ours.

The brawny woman is all business, scowling like a Russian version of nurse Ratchet from the movie *One Flew Over the Cuckoo's Nest*, and she stops next to the director of the baby house. She waits for a signal from the director who nods and the women holding the baby shouts at us in a quick burst of consonants.

Natasha says, "Is the Carter's baby," where Carole impulsively releases her death grip on Dave and skips across the room to retrieve her new baby boy.

The Carters are now across the room. I can see that their boy is a couple of months older than Dmitry. I whisper to Rick, "What do you think?" I tilt my head at Carole and baby Carter.

"What am I supposed to think?"

"Is it me or is there something strange about the way he smiles?"

"The baby, you mean?" Rick says.

"That expression, there, you see it? It's more adult than child."

"Sharon."

"He's too calm," I whisper.

"He's grown up here. That look on his face, my guess, it's a coping mechanism. When he's afraid or uncertain or whatever, he puts on the calm face and doesn't draw any attention to himself."

"He's two and a half."

"These kids grow up fast."

We meet our boys, our anxiety heightened by the fact that Dmitry was initially forgotten, or misplaced. During our time with them Sergey is an angel, Dmitry howls but totally wins our hearts with his tenacity. We fall in love with them instantly. Our little family parked on the floor of a baby house in Novokuznetsk, admiring and getting to know each other. Rick is holding Sergey and I have Dmitry. This is our first time with the boys. For a brief second, I let myself marvel at how long this journey has been, from when I met Rick all the way through three IVF treatments and one near-death experience. Dmitry's shrill cry brings me back to reality in Russia. I hug him and whisper soothing sounds in his ear. To no avail. He screams again. Eventually he stops, and to our amazement begins to dutifully pick up his toys. Our visit ends after about an hour, which seems to pass within minutes.

In the minivan ride home Carole Carter says, "Have you decided?"

"About what?"

"Are you going to take him?" she says, referring I assume to Dmitry who hadn't stopped hollering in a high-pitched howl the entire forty-eight minutes we were in his presence.

"Why wouldn't I?" I ask.

"Yes, of course. I just thought . . ."

I imagine I'm still holding Dmitry in my arms, crying as loudly as his little lungs will allow, and I grit my teeth. Who knows what a kid growing up in a place like this thinks? Who knows how his mind works or how he copes?

Dmitry has issues all right. He's a screamer. What's the big deal? Besides, it's nothing a loving home won't cure; in fact, it's exactly the sort of orphanage-induced can of worms adoption is supposed to cure. Dmitry had been rejected for adoption before and no way am I about to make his average two for two. The reason for rejection number one: physical deformities the paperwork said, which makes absolutely no sense given that he isn't misshapen or flawed in any way that I can tell.

Much of the paperwork we received from the Russian end of things was incomplete, labyrinthine, or flat out wrong. But I suspect wrong for perfectly good reasons. Some clever soul has figured out that by listing a bucketful of maladies (like the checked box that indicated both boys had rickets, a bone deformity caused by lack of vitamin D, and which neither boy has) they would be less likely to be adopted by a Russian family, thus making them more available for Americans who are more willing to accept (and smother with love, I might add) babies with all kinds of kooky ailments.

Nobody tells you about the conflicting medical reports. You have to figure it out on your own.

Our boys are small. That's true enough. But Rick and I didn't see any signs of abuse. Nothing especially weird happening at the baby house. No duct tape marks across the mouth. No cigarette burn scars, half-hidden bloodstains, or gunshot residue on their clothes, though I suspect any weirdness would take place well out of sight of adoptive parents. For all my paranoia and suspicion, the baby house is what it appears to be—a cash-strapped rural orphanage doing the best it can—and the children there are no more screwed up than those at any other cash-strapped rural orphanage. Dmitry is a screamer. I can live with that. Sergey is loving. I can live with that, too.

On the way back to the hotel the Carters hint that accepting Dmitry could be a mistake. They're trying to help, supporting us, if in fact we decide to turn down a child who so desperately needs a home. Rick does most of the talking and it doesn't come to much. We've already decided.

We arrive at the hotel and Natasha tells us to be ready tomorrow morning to return to the baby house. Same time. Same place.

At nine that evening, Rick and I clomp downstairs to the hotel restaurant and again say "da." The dining room is depressingly empty. An American sits at a table by the wall, a rustic-type who earlier told us about a mall nearby, which we visited. It wasn't actually a mall but an outdoor market with several rickety wooden tables, mountains of lacquer boxes, *matryoshka* dolls, wool shawls, fur hats, hand-painted tea sets, wooden Christmas ornaments, decorative eggs, and amber brooches.

Our food arrives, two bowls filled with pastry dumplings with some kind of meat inside. I have a headache and I can't stop thinking about the boys. The dumplings are slathered in butter and I pick at them. Rick eyes the mayonnaise set on the table and thumbs his spoon, but doesn't actually touch his food.

In the morning we repeat the long journey back to the orphanage. I hand over our gifts to the director—baby clothes by the armful, sacks full of socks (apparently, Russian orphanages have a never-ending need for socks), and soft leather wallets with froufrou logos for the caregivers and several cashmere scarves, one for Natasha with indigo shading and fringed tassels, and another for the director with a crinkled finish in rose-petal-pink, and a third just in case somebody important shows up or we need to bribe our way out of an unpredicted Siberian pickle.

And disposable diapers.

The director is all smiles, ready to skitter backwards into her office and wrap up in her scarf. She motions Rick and I that-away with a little backhand gesture in the direction of the playroom where we stand waiting for fifteen minutes. Two women arrive, the first, a chubby matron with wrestler's forearms carrying Sergey, and a shorter woman cradling a freshly scrubbed and polished Dmitry ready for viewing. Dmitry's lungs are operating at full capacity, his stuffed bear gripped in both hands daring anyone to pry it loose.

Our hour lasts for exactly forty-six minutes. The same two women return, scoop up the boys and march down the hall. The director is waiting in the hall and she blah blahs with Natasha who says, "Is time. Please come with me."

Natasha hustles us into the director's office, a dismal space with aging, wood-grained office furniture. The director looks up at us and shows her graying teeth. No sign of the scarf.

Even now, after two visits with the boys, I'm nervous, secretly fearful something ominous and unexpected will squelch the deal. The whole Russian-baby-adoption thing was a giant real-life crapshoot. You get a couple photos of these cute little guys and you decide to take a chance. You snag last minute flights from New York to Moscow to Novokuznetsk. If you don't like what you find when you get there, you've just wasted a lot of money and time and you get the thrill of starting all over.

"She wants to know," Natasha says, "do you want the boys?"

"Do I want them?" I say, pausing, appreciating the importance of the moment.

"You must say for the record."

"Of course I want them."

"She says yes." Natasha speaks this in English to the director who nods and writes something on a fleshy pink form.

Natasha looks from the director to me. "And Dmitry?"

I glance at Rick, and he nods. "Dmitry, yes. We want both boys."

"Okay, sign here and here, and their names you put here."

I sign and sign. I write in neat bold letters their new names: Hunter Sergey Simons and Dylan Dimitry Simons. The names are Rick's idea—Dylan after Bob Dylan, the singer/songwriter, and Hunter after Hunter S. Thompson, the journalist/writer. Rick signs and we all smile, shake hands, and say our goodbyes. Within minutes we are standing outside the baby house.

Just before we climb into the minivan, I ask Natasha to ask the director, hell, beg her, to put the boys in the same playgroup. I don't fully understand the grouping criteria, if there even is one (and I secretly suspect it's no more complicated than eeny-meeny-miny-moe), but for whatever reason Hunter and Dylan are in different groups, and in fact had never met before yesterday, so we were told.

Natasha ambles back inside with little or no zing in her step, and returns seconds later. To me it seems she was inside just long enough to count to three, comment on the weather to anyone standing nearby, possibly actually speak to the director, though unlikely, and convey what a snazzy scarf the director has wrapped around her neck and then hustle back outside.

"What'd she say?" I ask.

"Nyet." Natasha shakes her head slowly, eyes down like a surgeon delivering bad news.

End of discussion. I'm too exhausted to argue. I feel a wave of helplessness wash over me, not to be able to support or provide for our boys while we travel back home and wait to return for them.

Chapter Seventeen

The Long Wait

··

Our next step: we aim for home.

We board one of Siberian Air's doddering airplanes, an aging Airbus A319 with a spiffy new paint job, for the six-hour flight from Novokuznetsk to Moscow. Long before we defy gravity and soar away, we sit on the runway inside what feels like a giant green lame duck. The newly painted limey green airplanes are meant to scream newness, customer loyalty, and global commerce (not be confused with on time departures, technological advances, and air safety.) Rick elbows me and points his chin out the window. "What do you figure that's all about?"

I see a small gathering of people huddled on the ground outside our airplane—a pilot and copilot, three flight crew, four, no, five men with scruffy faces and large bellies who must be mechanics or baggage handlers—all bunched together at the base of the stairs like a pack of grade-schoolers up to no good.

"I'm sure it's nothing," Rick says.

"Or we're part of a disaster waiting to happen," I say.

A year earlier, a Siberia Airlines Airbus A310 crashed on landing at the Irkutsk International Airport. (This was an ancient seventies A310 and not the newer limey-green A319, so that's some consolation.) Rather than decelerate on landing, the big-thumbed pilot hit the wrong lever and accelerated sending the nearly thirty-year-old tin can whirling forward where it overran the runway by a wide margin, pulverized a concrete barrier doing sixty mph, and promptly burst into flames. One hundred and twenty-four people gone.

Outside on the tarmac a man wearing one of those delightful one-piece mechanic's outfit that shows off his belly raises a fist and points at the pilot and shouts and points some more. His finger gets inches and half inches from the pilot's chest without actually touching anything.

"It's probably routine," Rick says. "One of those pre-flight conference things."

"You think so?"

I lean across Rick's lap and put my nose to the window, getting as close to the action as possible, hoping that my inquiring presence will hurry things along. The pilot and crew argue for an excruciatingly long time, meanwhile more crew does repeated inspections up and down the aisle.

"Are we idiots for staying on the plane?"

"Idiots sounds a bit strong," Rick says. "Naïve maybe. Dumb trusting Americans, that could be us."

As Rick and I debate the merits of sitting tight verses skedaddling, a couple of bruisers up front get into a fist fight, apparently a regular happening for Siberia's Moscow-Novokuznetsk loop. I get a good view of the action this time, as one gets punched in the face hard enough for me to hear the fleshy smack a fist makes against a rather large nose. The man with the now bloody nose, stumbles backwards but doesn't fall, or cuss, or complain in any way. He cups his nose and shakes his head like the blow might have loosened something, steps forward, sits in his seat, and snaps his seat belt in place. End of fight. No words. No lifted eyebrows. Outside, back on the ground, another body heads off to the terminal building, this time a mechanic. Rick keeps his head to the window. "You'd think they'd have a golf cart or something as much as these guys walk back and forth."

About the time I've lost interest in the comings and goings of pilots, aircraft mechanics and cabin crew and begin fretting about leaving the boys in their dreadful environment. Finally someone, I can't see who, sends the stairs on wheels on its way and latches the door. We taxi, wait our turn, and lift off the ground for Moscow.

We land, visit the bathrooms, find a place to sit and proceed to kill the next four hours. The Carters wander by. Their time-killing strategy is to stay on the move. "Was it me," Carole says, "or was that weird?"

"It could have been worse," I say.

"Sitting on the runway like that, I couldn't take it. I wanted off."

"It wasn't so bad," Dave says.

She glares at Dave. "You try standing on a ledge twenty stories up," she says. "That's what it felt like to me. I'm twenty stories off the ground and there I am standing on a ledge."

"It's over now," Dave says.

"Dave had to talk me down," Carole says. "I felt like I could fall or jump or who knows what. But he talked me down."

We chat a little more, then say our goodbyes.

We board our next flight, Aeroflot Airlines, Moscow to the John F. Kennedy Airport. For the next nine hours, we sit on our butts and spend much of the time thinking about the boys. We land, lug bags to the car, drive home, unpack. At daybreak the next morning, I set about planning for the day the boys will arrive.

Chapter Eighteen

Planning

··

I call a painter, a muralist really, and have him haul his artistic wit and brushes over to River Drive and get to work. He does one room in a racetrack theme, all four walls filled with colorful race cars surrounded by race fans in silhouette and above them, clouds and helicopters (not exactly recreating a day at the races, but I think the boys will like it nonetheless). I'm thrilled with the result and talk him into coming back to do another room. I'd originally thought of putting both boys in one room—my two buddies growing up together side by side—but once I see the room in full bloom I think they each need their own mural.

In some ways, I'm terrified of over planning, near panic-stricken that the very act of preparing will somehow botch the deal. I've grown accustomed to aiming high and getting naught for my efforts except loss—the *in vitro* processes (all three of them), the pregnancies (both of them), the near death experience (only one of those), In each case, I had been cruising merrily along, life going smoothly, when without my notice, the orderliness and grandness of things vanished, the rhythm of life altered, the oomph all but gone. The worst part?

I never saw any of it coming. In truth, I hadn't even considered that I might run smack into a catastrophe that was way bigger than me, bigger than Rick and me together. Now, however, I understand the possibility of loss. Got it. Things don't always go as planned. Got it. Life isn't fair. Got it. Even a good life can go to hell. Ditto.

For all my planning, I manage to hold off on buying furniture, just in case.

On Thursday I pull out my cell phone and reconnect with Ally at the agency. I tell her about the visit to Russia, the mishaps, oddity, and adventure of travel in a strange land. Though I'm anxious and impatient for some decision about the boys, Ally is not. She's all optimism and laughs, pacifying me with giggles and a soothing patience. She reminds me that once I signed the paperwork at the baby house, the documents were whisked off to a provincial administrative center in Kemerovo, 120 miles north of the baby house, where an overworked bureaucrat will bless the transaction, or not, and put us on the docket to go before the judge who will give the official A-okay. Or not.

"Don't worry," Ally says, "we do everything we can to assure the adoptees are well taken care of."

"The adoptees?" I ask.

"The boys, I mean."

"Dylan and Hunter," I say.

"Dylan and Hunter, of course." Ally is easygoing and solid at the same time, like the barges rolling down the Nanticoke River reassuring you with their regularity. She has the ability to intuitively choose the path of least resistance and avoid making things harder than they could be.

"How long will it take?" I ask.

"Most parents wait four weeks," Ally says. "Up to eight."

"But it could be longer?"

"Yes," she says quietly. "It could be longer."

"I miss the boys already."

"I know you do."

Ally e-mails or calls every few days with requests for more information, more signed paperwork, assurances, proof, none of it official until stamped with a formal seal by a range of U.S. agencies. Ally is only the messenger, though this fact doesn't prevent me from griping about these last minute requests. "Huh? Explain that to me," I say, which she does for the thousandth time. The real culprit, the man behind the random requests, is in Kemerovo, someone who I will never hear from directly, never see and have no way of contacting, all for good reason.

In August 2007, Ally telephones. Her tone is especially lulling. She's all mumbly, like a priest at your bedside moments before you croak. A bad sign. She explains that another faceless nobody at the Kemerovo court is "concerned" that Rick and I have been married only a year and a half ago.

"Oh My God, can he possibly deny us our babies?" I say.

"Well," Ally says, "he possibly can, it is his duty to choose an appropriate home for the children...."

The next thing I do is hang up and find a chair where I bawl like a baby for the better part of three hours until Rick gets home from the hospital.

"It's over," I say blubbering away, wiping my nose with the back of my shirtsleeve. "This man, whoever he is, he hates us."

"We can get past this," Rick says, which is just the sort of thing he would say, the sort of thing he would always say when he comes face-to-face with a brick wall, or sandstone, or whatever they build walls out of in Siberia. This scene, me upset and Rick comforting me, is sobering. It touches off a moment of real doubt, a moment when for the first time, I get a whiff of a possible catastrophe coming my way. The moment of doubt feels sure and unyielding so that it no longer qualifies as doubt, but an unsettling moment of unconditional certainty. All my effort, all the money and travel, all my longing, preparation, and two perfectly good racecar murals, for chrissakes, is no match for the collective bureaucracy of the Kemerovo court system. They win. We lose.

The boys lose.

This is all in my head, of course, but what's not in my head is the pang of loss. That's occurring low, about belt height, sharp and pointed. It hurts and it's real.

Rick tugs off his jacket and gently lays it across the back of my chair. "The man simply asked a question, is all," Rick says. "We tell him that we were in love for years before we married or we say something else. We tell him the truth."

"It's not that easy," I say.

"Or we tell him what he wants to hear," he says, resigned, "I'm not really sure it matters. What matters is that we answer as quickly as possible, that we keep things moving." Rick is standing over me looking down. He is tired and worn out. I can see it in his eyes, the furrow in his brow, the worry lines all bunched up at odd angles and more visible than they should be for a man of fifty-two who keeps himself in stomach-crunching shape and who for all practical purposes is a man who doesn't worry. Much. He's been at the hospital eight, ten hours, I forget. A long time to rush around fixing broken hearts and here he is at home, off the clock, doing his best to fix mine.

"They're looking for an excuse," I say.

"They?"

"They, he, what difference does it make?" I say. "For weeks he's tried to trip us up, to catch us in some transgression."

"They're merely trying to do their job."

Rick is right and deep down I know it, but I'm still stressing.

I march off to my room (our room), lie down, then rise and stretch and sit down at my laptop and write yet another letter explaining things—that Rick and I are deliriously in love, stable and happy. That we are as committed to this marriage and our adopted children as a pair of swans, mated for life.

Chapter Nineteen

Trip #2, Delaware
to Kemerovo

·······································

I n late August I get the call from Ally. "We have a court date," she says.

I can't believe it. "When?" I ask.

"Monday, September third."

"A week from now, you mean?"

"That's why I called. You need to prepare."

The flight is a slumberous nine hours with an eight-hour layover in Moscow followed by a six-hour jaunt on to Kemerovo. On the final leg or our journey, I memorize the itinerary.

Day 1 – Depart USA

Day 2 – Arrive Moscow/ depart to Kemerovo

Day 3 – Arrive Kemerovo

Day 4 – Court appearance and paperwork

Day 5 – Pick up adoptees

Day 6 – Depart Kemerovo to Moscow

Day 7 – Take boys to medical appointment

Day 8 – Obtain visas for boys

Day 9 – Register visas

Day 10 – Wait for registration approval

Day 11 – Wait for registration approval

Day 12 – Return to USA as a family.

We land in Kemerovo on Sunday, six a.m. It's sixty degrees and rainy.

We check into a hotel where we meet another American couple awaiting their court appearance. The couple, the Coxes, are from Jersey. She is a large heavy woman, a nurse who can't stop talking even as her husband, a computer guy, politely interrupts her to give Rick and I a chance to say boo. When that doesn't do the trick, he takes her by the arm as she's speaking and guides her down the hallway out of earshot.

That said, we are still fellow soon-to-be-adoptive-parents-in-Kemerovo—meaning that the Coxes and we are instantly bonded so thoroughly that even non-stop talking can't drive us apart. The four of us talk and worry, in the hotel lobby, stroll up and down grimy streets waiting for our day in court.

On Labor Day, September 3, 2007, our interpreter for this leg of the journey, Galina, picks us all up at the hotel. She drives us to a tiny, ornate Soviet-style courthouse whose gray façade looks pressed from a giant waffle maker. A couple of security guards in crumpled uniforms lean against the front wall giving the place a disheveled but nonetheless official aura.

Inside we pass several dark jail cells with floor to ceiling metal bars and thankfully no one inside.

They give me the creeps.

Rick, nothing fazes him. "That's how they do it here," he says.

"Like in an old movie," I whisper.

"They throw people in jail and when it's time, they yank them out and prop them in front of the judge." Rick shakes his head and presses his lips together into a thin horizontal line. "The whole thing's a sham." His tone is not so much angry as disappointed.

"Even more like a movie," I say.

"A kangaroo court."

"And if the judge says you're guilty?"

"They're always guilty," Rick says. "I read it somewhere. If you make it to court, you're guilty. Then off to Siberia."

"We are *in* Siberia."

"Northern Siberia where the temperatures are subarctic."

"I'm not going to ask what subarctic means," I say.

"Summers last about a week."

His voice carries an urgent logic. The bad guys get punished. The good guys get to adopt. Or at least that's what I imagine he's hinting at. For all his medical training, I can tell Rick is nervous on the inside where it doesn't show, gripped by the momentum of having to slog through such a place, a courthouse with jail cells and steel bars, wary of the thought that things might not go as planned, that our Russian judge might just say, "No way Jose."

I take his hand and whisper, "This conversation isn't making me feel any better."

"I'm sorry. I got carried away. It'll be all right."

We come to a wide corridor lined with scuffed metal chairs. The Coxes plop down on the chairs, put their hands in their laps and wait to be summoned. Mr. Cox is a really nice guy, but his choice of clothing for the proceedings causes us concern. Our paperwork said to dress nicely for court. Business casual, it said. He has on a striped collarless shirt, pleated pants with a studded belt, and black running shoes. Rick has on a suit, a dark navy, narrow striped, two button, and I'm wearing a two-piece pant outfit, navy and gray, what I imagine are the ideal colors to get on the good side of a Russian judge. Rick and I walk aimlessly down the corridor trying to occupy ourselves.

"I'm antsy, I just want everything to be perfect." I say.

"Take a deep breath," says Rick. Mrs. Cox says something speaking in decibels way too loud for normal conversation. I turn and whisper to Rick, "What if they go first? What if they say the wrong thing, wearing the wrong clothes, and it reflects on us?"

"That's not going to happen," Rick says.

He's right. Maybe I'm losing it. "Do we know the judge's name?"

"It's written somewhere. I can't pronounce it."

"What do we call him? Your Honor, is that appropriate?"

"Perfectly appropriate," Rick says and I wonder how he knows such things, how he has the moxie to make such pronouncements with such aplomb even when he's making it up. I've come to rely on Rick's poise. I've grown accustomed to having a man nearby who knows a lot about lots of things and when he doesn't know, his type of guessing—logical inference, deductive reasoning, however he comes up with these things— is second nature.

I say, "So what if Your Honor gets angry at *them* and takes it out on us?"

My husband widens his stance and brings the fingers of both hands together in front of him, tapping them lightly and begins one of his polite lectures. "Number one, we have followed the process exactly . . . " and later, " . . . unwanted babies . . ." and " . . . a national expense . . . off loading that expense." Finally he says, "We are reasonable people. I'm a doctor, for crying out loud. Why wouldn't they give us two babies?"

An impeccable logic, I'm sure, but one that has zero affect on a mother this close to taking possession of two beautiful blond, blue-eyed boys that she already considers her own. Rick is trying to console me with reasonableness, but I'm way too far gone to listen. When our interpreter abruptly stands and asks who wants to go first, I blurt out, "We do. We do."

Galina checks her watch, stands a little taller, and brushes lint from her blouse, as if building up her courage to enter the courtroom, which makes me nervous as hell. I check my own blouse for lint, don't find any, and brush a speck of nothing from the sleeve of Rick's navy suit. I wonder now if asking who wanted to go first was a trick. Was the wise move to go last? Do Russian judges, or specifically those from Kemerovo, grow more lenient as the day wears on? Here I am standing in a corridor, nowhere near the courtroom and I'm already pleading for leniency. I'm jittery and scared. Versions of courtroom fiascos flick through my head. What if… what if I can't speak when spoken to? What if I get the courtroom version of stage fright? What if my voice box swells shut on me and my legs can't keep me upright? What if I field a tough game-ending question and rather than popping off a clever, slightly humorous response that puts everyone at ease, I sputter nonsensically and laugh hysterically?

Galina rolls her head around on her shoulders like a boxer about to enter the ring, looks left down the corridor then right. I half expect her to click her heels, salute, or some other crazy thing. "Is this way," she says and escorts us deeper into the building via a maze of hallways without jail cells and into a tiny room with walls the color of dry mud. Three somber judges, all women, which momentarily confuses me, sit behind a chipped and worn judges' bench of dark wood. The mood in the room is all business. One of the judges, a pink-faced woman with short red hair, sits on a raised platform in the center of the bench between the two other somberly robed women.

Directly in front of and facing the bench rests four metal folding chairs. We sit, Rick, me and Galina.

The center judge mumbles to her colleagues, then looks up and squints at us.

"The judge says welcome," Galina whispers, which isn't true because the judge hasn't yet spoken to us.

When the judge does open her mouth she uses a combination of Russian and convoluted English to make her point. Most of it we understand, but when things get dicey, Galina perks up.

"You are here," the judge says looking from Rick to me to Galina. "Good, we begin." She stares down at the paperwork in front of her. Without glancing up she asks a series of preplanned questions, first of Rick then of me. Do you have children? Have you ever taken care of children? Can you support a child, no, let's see here, two children? We take our turn and I do my best to stay in line with Rick's responses without exactly mimicking his answers and thus hope to exude a subtle message to our panel of judges that my husband and I are of one mind when it comes to childrearing.

The judge on the left leans in and whispers to the center judge who squints at her paperwork and flips through several pages of our fat adoption dossier. "You are newlyweds, no?"

Petrified, I blurt out, "We've known each other for some time."

"This some time," she says. "How many years?"

"Four," I say.

"And this is a stable marriage?"

"Absolutely," I say too quickly and in a shrill voice that screams liar. To make up for the pleading in my delivery, I pause, inhale through my nose and say, "We were made for each other." This I say in a dreamy lilt. "You know what I mean. We want to be together and we want children."

Rick, cool as a Russian winter, pats my leg and says, "We have a stable marriage, yes."

"And you are . . ." here the judge searches for just the right word, "mature," she says.

I open my mouth ready to give the judge the inside story on youth and maturity at the Simons' house, when the woman raises a hand in a stop-before-you-say-something-stupid gesture, which I do. The judge plods through our dossier page by page moving her entire head left to right, top to bottom, using her judge's x-ray eyes to pinpoint inconsistencies, searching for bright spots and air shadows, any indication that Rick and I are swindlers out to hoodwink an unsuspecting province out of its unwanted babies. She lifts each sheet of paper with the fingers of one hand and meticulously places it upside down on top of the small pile forming to the right of the larger pile in front of her. She asks about our finances. She questions our pay stubs. She turns pages, looks and pauses. She raises an eyebrow and lifts a stapled bundle of papers in the air so that we can see what she's seeing—our tax returns for the last two years, it turns out—and she asks us to swear the information is correct. What she actually says is, "You pay this much in taxes, is it true?"

"She asks if the information authentic," Galina interprets.

Galina is about to reinterpret when Rick says, "The information is accurate, Your Honor." He nonchalantly makes eye contact with each of the three judges one at a time. The judge purses her lips and nods several times, but I sense this isn't the nod of "I agree with you," or "It's all perfectly clear," but some other kind of Russian nod that spells trouble. The judge continues to nod and rocks back and forth in her chair, taking forever to puzzle over our taxes. She peers down at Rick and at me and I'd swear she's about to say something grave, but in the end doesn't say anything.

Next, she lifts Rick's passport, scans the tiny pages for anything unsavory and riffles to the last sheet where a gummy yellow Russian visa has been neatly cemented in place. She squints at it and runs two fingers across the yellow paper, presumably a woman who can ferret out a forgery by touch, hands the passport to one of the other judges who does a second quick finger inspection and hands the document back. She spends an eternity examining my passport, searching, I imagine, for the appropriate stamps and dates. She places the passports upside down on her right and reads our marriage certificate, at one point smiling and mumbling to the judge on her left. She reads our medical charts, letters from our doctors vouching that Rick and I won't cease breathing anytime soon, and letters from the pediatrician we contacted and plan to visit within days of landing on U.S. soil.

And on it goes for the better part of an hour.

The last item on the agenda is the waiting period. As a rule the judge will require a two-week waiting period during which we can't take the boys out of Siberia. The rationale for the two week wait isn't clear, but neither is much of the adoption process. What this means is that for two weeks, we and the boys are stuck in a hotel somewhere close, Novokuznetsk or Kemerovo. In an effort to make life easy on everyone, we had submitted a formal request to waive the waiting period. "It happens," Ally told us in a leery voice.

Before we get to the waiver there is one last thing. The judge stares at Rick. "You agree for an appointed agency to visit the boys?"

"We look forward to the visits," Rick says.

"Once per year. You are aware of this requirement?"

"As often as they like."

"Very well," she says. "You will wait outside, please."

Ten minutes later we shuffle back into the courtroom where the judge pronounces, in Russian, which of course we don't understand until Galina works her magic and spits out the words, that she grants our application to adopt *and* we have the green light to dash off to America as soon as we complete the remainder of our agenda.

"Congratulations," the judge says or something like it.

The flat lighting now seems much brighter.

"Spasiba," I say loudly and repeatedly, and don't even try to hold back the tears.

Chapter Twenty

Paperwork and Poop

Rick and I take our seats in the courthouse corridor, wait an agonizing sixty minutes, and finally see the Coxes bounding our way giddy as high schoolers, apparently given the nod from the judge.

A few minutes later, Galina says, "The fathers we take to see the police. The mothers, you return to the hotel." This she says from the front seat of the minivan where the temperature is 1,000 degrees, the windows are open, the breeze is sweltering, and the road noise is making it hard to hear. Galina anticipates my objection to Rick going one way and me and the chatty Mrs. Cox going another, and when I open my mouth, which Galina can't possibly see, she raises a hand and says, "The men must sign the papers. You will wait at the hotel."

This is where life speeds up a notch or two. I can't describe the movement properly because it's partly in my head—me thinking of sprinting to see my two small boys all alone in some back room of the baby house, the caregivers knowing the boys are short-timers, possibly paying them less attention, using up what energy they have on the dozens (could be tens of dozens for all I know) remaining orphans.

Our driver bolts through yellow-turning-red lights, gunning the poor overworked motor until it screams for a reprieve, and passes cars and generally makes the ride as menacing and unpleasant as possible. We cruise along the M-53 swerving from lane to lane, passing slower cars, and I see street names like Lenin, and Kosarev whiz by. We reach the hotel where the driver slows and then skids to a stop, not in the hotel driveway where you'd expect, but on the street out front, and where Mrs. Cox and I are unceremoniously dumped.

Rick shows up two hours later, tired, mildly irritated at something or someone but refuses to say, and when I pester him for details he plops down hard onto the bed, a great weight lifted, and leans back until he is stretched out flat on his back. He says, "Look at this," and hands me a thick packet of official-looking paperwork with elaborate red seals stamped in the upper right of each page. "No", he says. "On the bottom. There." Underneath all the paperwork are two temporary passports. "Look inside," he says. "At the names. Go ahead and read them."

I open the first passport and stare.

"Read it aloud."

"Hunter Sergey Simons," I say.

"And the other."

I turn the flap of the other passport. It feels plastic and unreal against my fingers.

"Go on," he says.

My husband breathes in and out and stares at the ceiling, a man exhausted, but at the same time letting himself be restored, rejuvenated by the power of words.

"Please," he says. We both wait a beat.

"Dylan Dimitry Simons." I read it and cry.

That evening, we have dinner in a small restaurant not far from the hotel, a relaxed place with a band in the corner and a woman belting out a series of jazz numbers in English and who sounds terrific. The food is good; we discuss during the meal our impressions of Siberia. There is a pervasive look and feel of poverty and bleakness but despite this the people seem decent, hardworking, handsome, and friendly. The infrastructure is dated, almost primitive, think America in the 1950's. And there is plenty of land.

Kemerovo is a good four hours from the orphanage by minivan, a long drive made longer by Mrs. Cox's constant prattling and her tendency to laugh after every inane comment. "Boy, these roads are narrow. He-he-he." We again endure the driving (which by now we've almost become accustomed to) and manage to enjoy the countryside. We arrive at the orphanage and the four of us rush inside, Galena behind. We wait for the staff to bring our children. I reach for Dylan who leans into me and then starts into his usual wail and I've no idea what it is he's trying to tell me. Since we met, he hasn't said a word, but only wails in a sort of rhythm, a pattern, possibly a song or nursery rhyme he memorized and sings the only way he knows how. Both Dylan and Hunter have been dolled up, cleaned and pressed for the big day they get sprung from the baby house. Hunter, now clutching at Rick's ear, is simultaneously hugging the stuffed bear we gave him on our first visit.

A large woman with a baby girl in her arms trudges over to the Coxes, hands off the bundle and, thus completing her delivery, marches silently away. The girl's features look Asian, a smooth face and high cheekbones. The Coxes squeeze and snuggle and coo their precious baby girl, Isabella, who for her part appears as pleased as punch to be adopted. Mr. Cox nudged out his wife and took hold of the girl right away and now has tears streaming down his face and dripping onto the sleeve of his shirt, holding Isabella close to his face, mumbling into her tiny ear. Most of what he says I can't hear, but some I can.

"I'll never leave you," he whispers. "Not ever. I'll tell you right now, little one, I will never, ever leave you. You'll never be alone again—"

"Alone," Mrs. Cox says, "I'll bet she's dying for a little alone time after spending a few months with this bunch here."

Watching these two—Mr. Cox and Isabella, Mr. Cox and Mrs. Cox—is a powerful and strange moment, the big strong man going to pieces and the talkative wife rationalizing those emotional pieces back into place and the baby taking it all in from the comfort of her new father's arms.

Rick and I are grinning ear to ear, trying not to be overwhelmed by the moment. There is not enough time to reflect or rejoice. The room is swirling with emotions and activity. I manage to hand someone my camera and they snap photos with Rick and me and the boys and several of the caregivers and Galina and the director. When that's done I hand over more disposable diapers to the director, four large bundles, as a sort of standard departing donation.

I get my baby boys; the baby house gets a batch of diapers and a genuine thank you.

Meanwhile Dylan is howling, hanging onto his own stuffed bear. One of the caregivers, an old woman with a weathered face and wearing a pair of retro black Converse high-tops reaches for Dylan and with deft hands strips him of his cute little jumper faster than I can say, "Here, let me help."

Russia trip with boys

"Nyet," the woman says because she's already completed the job and she reaches for Hunter who holds up both arms, not in the least afraid of her, but obeying a command before it's given, and in half a second he's naked down to his diaper.

We have with us a fresh set of baby clothes— matching outfits perfect for two brothers a blue polo shirt and khaki pants. The clothes are way too big, ginormous is more like it. The boys are sixteen and twenty-three months, but small for their age. We knew that, so we bought clothes for a twelve month old, which are still too big. We dress them in the oversized outfits, say quick goodbyes, and with a minimum of fanfare slip out the door.

Outside is hot as a Saharan desert.

Galina says, "Where are their hats?"

"Hats," I say and at the same time try to figure out what she could possibly mean.

"The boys," Galina says. "They must have hats, no?"

I glance up at the sky then back at Galina, beads of perspiration on her forehead.

Now that I think if it, every Siberian child I'd seen since arrival was sporting a hat of some kind, imitation military fur hats, wool hats or floppy-eared leather hats. I tell her I'll look into rustling up some hats first chance I get.

On the way back to Kemerovo, sans car seats and seatbelts and hats, Rick and I grip onto the boys like human life preservers. Yegor is mad to get out of town and the moment we hit the road both boys begin to cry and cry. And cry. We try talking and singing and bouncing and hugging and dazzling them with cute red hammers we brought along for just such circumstances. Nothing works. An hour into the drive, we stop at a small roadside store and Rick buys a couple of bottles of apple juice, a food item we were told the boys had guzzled in large quantities since birth and just the thing for the long drive. Galina suggests we mix the juice with water, the best idea she's had yet, and Rick concocts a fifty-fifty potion of watery apple juice. He pours the mixture into two separate bottles and passes each child their own bottle that they grab hold of and sip at first and then suck with great force until the bottles make noisy slurping sounds.

We drive and the boys suck on their bottles. We fill the bottles and wait for more bubbly noises. Two hours into the drive both boys come down with the worst case of diarrhea in recorded history. The smell is bad. We pull over and I change diapers. The stink surfaces again fifteen minutes later and the driver says something to Galina, a catch in his voice. Galina ratchets her body around and looks at the boys, Dylan in my lap and Hunter in Rick's arms. She scrunches up her nose and makes a noise that sounds nothing like it but what I hear is, "Pee-yew."

As for the source of said stink, Rick reminds me it could be carsickness, stress, adoption anxiety, or something in the air. Blaming the apple juice for all the pooping never once occurred to us.

Once in our hotel room, I demand from my husband the doctor a firm diagnosis with little or no waffling and no maybes and no we'll-just-have-to-wait-and-sees. Rick explains it's probably a virus (but in hindsight the apple juice may have contributed). Given that the boys are losing fluids faster than we can fill them up, Rick tells me it's critical that we hydrate them. "Now," he says, "and ongoing." What we have as our primary source of hydration is more diluted apple juice which we ply them with on a regular schedule, the same schedule we use for changing diapers, about every twenty minutes it turns out. In between changes, we set the boys on the carpeted floor. Dylan determinedly cruises off, exploring on all fours. Hunter tries to crawl, his skinny arms and legs wavering pitifully. He stops after a few feet and looks up at us, smiling, happy. In that moment I fall in love all over again. I know that past hardships, and those still to come, are worth it. The boys are meant for us. And us for them.

Chapter Twenty-One

The Day After

·······································

A fter an absorbing first night, the boys crying and likely starved for something that sticks in their small tummies. The four of us get up at four a.m., take turns showering and wiping away fresh poo and getting dressed and finally wriggling our way into our new baby carriers, cute little frontpack jobs with a pouch chest high and the perfect size for a former Russian orphan. Once inside, the boys squirm and kick and grab for a handhold but eventually settle in for the ride. I take Hunter because he's lighter and Dylan goes with Rick. As a test, I bend forward and see if my little sixteen-month-old boy, about the size of a large cantaloupe, falls out of my frontpack. Everything A-okay. Next, I reach down and grab the handle of one of the suitcases. With my remaining free hand, I grip my purse, filled with several heavy Russian dymkovo toys - clay figurines of dancing bears, horses, and painted chickens; part souvenir, part airplane flight playthings.

In all our gallivanting across the Russian Federation we discover that Russian airline travelers wrap their luggage in plastic. Who knows why exactly, but it strikes us as a good idea even if I don't fully appreciate the benefits, so out from Rick's bag he pulls an extra large roll of Home Depot plastic wrap and we get to it, swaddling our three bags so thoroughly they appear bombproof.

With Hunter hanging from my neck, luggage in one hand, and loaded purse in the other, I tell myself this will work. Not for the long slog up Mount Elbrus (the highest mountain in Russia), but for the walk down stairs to the lobby, across the lobby and out the door, into the waiting minivan, and at least two rest stops, it will work.

With our boys firmly pressed to our chests and our luggage safely water tight to fifty meters, we load up and let Galina and Yegor zip us along to the Kemerovo Airport.

The airport is wall-to-wall bodies and baggage and airport helpers being as unhelpful as possible, though most are immaculately dressed. Before we reach the counter the Siberian Air worker in a trim, dark blue ensemble and white gloves steps in front of us, glares down at the largest of our freshly plastic-wrapped bags, says something foreign that doesn't sound remotely Russian, and quickly produces a blade of some kind, slices through our plastic wrap along the zipper, and proceeds to rummage through our belongings. He does this while issuing what sound like orders and generally giving us a hard time. Hunter, ensconced in his pouch in front of me is surprisingly quiet through all this, but as a consolation prize stinks like a little boy with way too much apple juice inside him and a nasty case of diarrhea that at this very moment is oozing out the sides of the diaper and down one of his legs.

Rick is frantic, meaning that he is standing motionless to one side scanning the area for our interpreter. Lucky us, Galina isn't too far away, gazing, mesmerized at a food kiosk where she is considering the pros and cons of a jelly donut.

After a fair amount of arm waving, Galina arrives, schmoozes the white gloved baggage inspector and convinces him to go harass someone else. My new challenge (in addition to entertaining a sixteen-month-old with poop dripping down his legs) is to get all of our belongings to fit back into the suitcase they just came out of. This, as anyone knows, is physically impossible when attempted while standing at the departure counter of a crowded airport with hundreds of impatient foreign speaking travelers glaring at you to get a move on—several of the onlookers a dead knockoff of President Vladimir Putin, a man whose facial features connote unending impatience. What once fit inside our largest bag no longer does and I end up tossing several pieces of perfectly good clothing just to get the lid to latch. As for rewrapping our possessions, it isn't happening.

Next we check bags, change diapers—twice in one sitting because Hunter decides to loosen his tiny bowels in mid-diaper change—and scrub myself for anything brownish, anything vaguely poopy looking until I'm clean as can be, though patchy with moisture. All goes as planned for the next thirty feet. When we reach the security gate, a uniformed man, flushed and hoarse, who must live to find fault, reviews our documents and doesn't like what he sees.

"This is wrong form," he says.

"How can that be?" Rick asks.

"This stamp here is missing."

"If I understand you," Rick says, casually holding Dylan in one arm as if he's light as a feather, and trying out his doctor's voice, "it's the right form but without the correct arrival stamp? Is that right?"

"Does not help to get upset," the man says, now staring at Hunter and me.

"But it is stamped," Rick says, "here and here, you see."

"You did not stay another day?"

"Yes, we stayed several."

"Okay, then you cannot proceed without the appropriate stamps."

Apparently, this scuffed piece of paper we've been hauling around with us was supposed to be date stamped for each day of our stay at the hotel. On arrival, the clerk took the paper and proceeded to pound on it with the stamp, over and over until I'd guess we had close to a dozen stamps somewhere on the page. Nobody said squat about a new stamp each day, so naturally we're a few stamps short.

I step in front of Rick and look up at the uniformed man. I say, "Is there anything you can do?"

"This day," the man says pointing at the paper, "is missing stamp."

Rick edged away from the man, hinting that he might just leave the security area and make a run for it (a clear violation of airport security protocol would be my guess). He stands on his tippy toes and catches sight of Galina still eyeing the donut stand. He waves her over, and Galina and the man in his uniform yammer back and forth for fifteen minutes until the man grudgingly gives in.

"Is okay to board the plane," he says. "Have nice flight."

We board our Siberian Airlines flight, locate our seats, buckle up, and Rick and I stare at each other not saying a word, both wondering which boy (my guess is Dylan) will soil his britches first. I win. Dylan makes a noisy mess, grunting and squawking like a maimed bird and when he's done I apologize to the man on my left for the smell and the sound effects. I whisper that there may be the tiniest bit of poo on the armrest and he ought to watch out. Before we get off the tarmac I whisk Dylan away to the bathroom, make a quick change and hustle back to my seat.

In the air things get worse. The boys' insides get loosened up and they pee and poop at will, conceivably with no bowel or bladder control whatsoever. To make matters worse they squirm in our arms, which has the affect of wrinkling their little plastic diapers in ways that open up cracks between diaper and leg and thus allow unpleasant fluids to dribble out and down their legs and onto their arms and onto our clothes. Did I mention the stink? Thirty minutes into the flight ten rows fore and aft of us the smell is strongest; think anchovies squirming out of their little cans. An hour into the flight, the entire cabin is engulfed in an indescribably funky stench.

At some point I run out of unsoiled diapers. Then I run out of unsoiled clothes. This it ten minutes prior to touch down and I decide to wrap my naked boys, one at a time, in blankets and pray this nightmare ends soon. The blankets don't stop them from crapping or stinking or crying, but I do manage to wrap them in such a way that the goo doesn't get on other passengers.

When we touch down in Moscow, the flight crew rushes us off the airplane and then crams the four of us, along with hundreds of other passengers, onto several buses and cart us, cattle like, from the airplane to the terminal building in the far distance. Rick and Dylan get shoved into a corner. I stand on the bus, one hand on a sturdy metal pole to keep me from tumbling head first into anyone, and one hand on the blanket-wrapped Hunter tucked inside the baby pouch (now weighing on me like an anchor), and one foot firmly on my purse/carry-on luggage combo.

We land on Thursday, September 6, 7:55 a.m., and as quickly as humanly possible, while carrying two poo-stained boys—who coincidently smell like a Jersey landfill—locate our Moscow interpreter, Yana, and our new driver (Yegor 4, if you're counting) who cart the seven of us, four adult Americans and our three Russian adoptees, into Moscow. The boys are uncomfortable and fidgeting but we try to keep them occupied looking out the window. Long before we get to our hotel, Yegor swerves into a parking lot adjacent to an apartment complex and offloads the Cox family.

I feel a bit sad and uneasy about separating from the Coxes (and think semi-seriously about letting them stay with us, in our room at the Marriott, but I know there are rules against such chicanery). Besides, if the Cox family can survive the night we'll see them tomorrow, bright and early. This part of the adoption process is consummated in teams—medical exams, visa applications, Embassy I-600 forms to fill out, and taking possession of two mysterious sealed envelopes (one for each child) from the American Embassy. Oh, also you are not permitted to open these envelopes. I get all this from the agency's Trip 2 Instruction packet which is exhaustingly thorough and fastidiously confusing.

Our next stop, the Marriott Grand Moscow Hotel on Tverskaya Street.

We check in, haul our worn out butts up to our room, and think fervently about plopping face first onto the king sized, pillow-topped bed but the boys aren't in any mood to sleep. They are irritable and take turns fussing and crying. In fact, for the next eight days we are in Moscow, rest and sleep are minimal.

Call me clever, but prior to making trip #2, I had used my sales skills (along with oodles of Marriott rewards points) and cajoled a hotel clerk into upgrading our room to one on the executive level floor, where the hotel chef has a spread of food fit for a king or a pair of orphans, depending on how you look at it. The kids are probably starved. I do some serious recon of the delicacies down the hall. For the kids I bring back rolls and pirozhkis (little pastries stuffed with what looks like potatoes or cheese) and blini (think crepes) and for dessert morozhenoe (ice crème with fruit on top). For the adults I load up on shashlyk (kebabs of meat and vegetables) and pelmeni (pastry dumplings filled with meatballs).

Having our own little food court so close to the room is a godsend and so begins a habit of letting Hunter and his big brother Dylan taste a bit of food, decide if they like it or not, and if not try something else. Dylan, the more picky of the two, can smell some foods from eight feet away and know with absolute certainty that he hates it and hence won't let so much as a morsel anywhere near his mouth. On the rare occasion I am able to sweet-talk him into tasting a crumb of something he's already declared off limits, he tricks me by taking the bread, pastry, or pancake into his thin hand, hinting that the hand might move to mouth, and then flinging the morsel as far as his not yet muscled arm is capable of.

Rick points out a golf ball sized gob of bread in Hunter's cheek. "It's called pouching."

"He's hungry," I say already defending the boys.

"It's a survival tactic. Shove as much food into your mouth as will fit and store it way back in the cheeks, so no one can take it away from you."

That and we notice the boys are hiding food. We find pieces of bread throughout the hotel room, under a pillow, behind a chair, deep in the toe of one shoe, and I hope once we get them home and acclimated to an unlimited supply of nutrition, the pouching and hoarding will stop.

Meanwhile, it's business as usual at the poop factory. My job is to remove the diaper from boy A while Rick entertains boy B (to no avail), then I hand off boy A to Rick who carts him quickly into the shower, soaps him up, sprays him down, and dries him while I do the diaper removal thing on boy B, were we then trade boys and I rediaper boy A, and on it goes. We do this quickly, getting better and faster with each leg of the race, trying to stay one step ahead of the next poop.

Chapter Twenty-Two

The List

....

While the judge had given us the okay to leave whenever we wanted, what she actually meant was that we could take off anytime after meeting a long list of predeparture requirements.

Friday we dash off to the American Medical Center to have the boys tested for HIV and oh while you're here, how about we do a mock medical check exam? The pediatrician, Dr. Popov, is a funny man with a sandblast voice who tells us the kids are fine, and even if they aren't fine exactly they'll get better soon enough. "As loud as this one here can scream, how sick can he be?"

"About the diarrhea?" I ask.

"Is nothing to worry about," he says.

"Are you sure?"

"Love them. Is all they need."

When we stroll out to the waiting room, the Cox family is standing at the reception desk, a tight little knot of anger and frustration, complaining to Yana in one of those extremely loud hushed-yells. Yana in turn is talking quietly to the receptionist. The issue is fifty dollars. Dr. Popov requested it for some vague last minute charge and the Coxes aren't willing to pay for one very good reason—they don't have it.

This little give and take goes on for some time, until I nudge Rick and whisper for him to do something.

"Like what?" he whispers back.

"Like something," I say.

Rick, cradling Dylan in his arms like an undersized football, saunters casually up to Mr. Cox and turns him away from his wife and says, "Any way I can help?"

"I planned for this," Mr. Cox says. "I really did. Not this, I mean, but we aren't irresponsible people."

"If you need anything," Rick says.

"That's not it," he says. "It's just…"

"Here," Rick says and reaches around with one hand to yank out his wallet, no small feat with Dylan in his arms, careful not to wake him and start the poor child on one of his screaming fits.

Mr. Cox sees what's happening and raises his arms putting a stop to things. "No," he says. "Completely unnecessary. I mean it. Absolutely, completely unnecessary."

Mrs. Cox gets wind of the secret negotiation. She says, "It's not right." I can see tears in her eyes. She glances at Isabella in her arms and then at me. "The doctor wants us to pay to fill out a form. Have you ever heard of such a thing? We have to pay him so we can scribble on some piece of paper."

"Look," Rick says. "Let me loan you a hundred, to cover anything else that might come up."

Ignoring the offer, Mr. Cox turns to Yana and asks about a cash machine, bank, anyplace to use a credit card to get some cash. She thinks about it, eyes scanning, and settles on two options. A store with a cash machine not far away and a distant option, a bank.

"How far is not too far?" Mr. Cox asks.

"Ten minutes," she says. "Come. I will take you."

The adoption agency crew has scheduled us with some task to perform every day, or nearly every day. But the weekend is all ours. Unfortunately the boy's bowel issues dominate our activities. We spend a lot of time wandering through the hotel, so to be able to rapidly return to our room as nature calls (and she calls quite often). Despite this we are getting to know our boys, and they us. Dylan and Hunter's personalities, even as infants, are becoming clearer to us. We are working through the food and sleep dilemmas. The boys test us but we smother them with love and affection, trying in the only way we can to recover them from (we imagine) years of neglect. We wish we knew more Russian words and phrases to help us connect.

On Sunday one of the hotel staffers takes mercy on us and loans us a double stroller, nearly begs us to take the thing. Get out of the hotel, explore Moscow, the staffer says. We noticed that Dylan hasn't spoken since the baby house, possibly even before that for all we knew. From his younger brother, we weren't expecting any chitchat, but Dylan, at twenty-three months, should have something to say. Once outside and within a block of the hotel, Dylan breaks out into a Russian song, most likely a nursery rhyme. It's music to our ears. As for exploring, we only make it a few blocks before we encounter an obstacle. To cross Moscow's main thoroughfares, massive six-lanners, pedestrians ease down steps on this side of the road and climb the corresponding stairs on the other side. At our first underpass, we stop and gaze around awkwardly like tourists. Rick is in the slow process of unstrapping Dylan when a well-dressed man in a fur hat offers by gesturing to help Rick carry the stroller down one side and up the other. Which they do.

When the man walks away, I look after him sort of expecting something weird—a hidden camera and a film crew posting strange but true travel videos to YouTube, a police officer ready to write us a ticket for who knows what. I say, "What just happened?"

"I'm not quite sure," Rick says.

"It's clear we're not in Manhattan."

Rick shakes his head. "No, I suppose we're not."

I feel safe in Moscow, not altogether surprising given the number of police and uniformed military patrolling the streets.

That evening I review an e-mail I had received from Ally from the adoption agency. The fee for an adoption Immigrant Visa is $380 per child. She highly recommends payment via credit card. She also includes a note about Part 204.3 of the Code of Federal Regulations which specifies that if we bring home two orphans who are not siblings, an additional fee of $670 is required for each orphan beyond the first. Now here's an unexpected expense. On Monday, we go to the Embassy and request visas for the boys.

The Embassy processes adoption visas two days a week and the experience is mostly about waiting. Move to room 101 and take a seat. Move to room 102 and take a seat. Each room is filled with Americans, many of them adopting.

Of the lot, only two other couples have adopted from Siberia; we are the only adopters with two children. To pass the time, I chat with several women. Rick shakes the men's hands, but they fidget and try not to look at each other for too long. Rick returns to his seat and leaves the chitchat to me. I'm taking a poll and so far, no one has had the ten-day waiting period waived. Everyone has a story, sometimes several stories. One women said her baby, Tia, a beautiful toddler with a full head of dark hair, was taken from her alcoholic mother when the mother passed out drunk in the middle of the street and little Tia was found fumbling in the road waiting for Mom to wake up. Another described the complications of living in Moscow with her child for two weeks after her husband flew home. Still another talked about the never-ending delays. Essentially all of us were exhausted, but deep down ecstatic about becoming parents and determined to see the process through.

Finally, it's our turn. We fill out more paperwork and answer the same questions we've answered a trillion times. A man standing in a cubicle behind a counter grants the boys their visas and hands Rick one brown envelope for each child. "Do not open," he says and smiles.

The following day, Tuesday, is a blur. We spend countless hours with the boys strolling around the hotel and making the occasional trip to the park (and nearby McDonalds) several blocks away.

In the brief moments when the boys are asleep and Rick or I have the energy to stay awake, we send a few e-mails to friends. We touch base with the Carter's, who as luck would have it, are scheduled for their court date a week after ours and are eager for details about the process. We send them our version of the ins and outs, ups and downs. Other friends receive less detailed accounts.

> From: Rick
> To: Mike & Julia
> Subject: From Russia
> Date: Saturday, September 8, 2007, at 11:22 AM
>
> Mike and Julia,
> Greetings from Moscow. We have the boys, most of the red tape done and anticipate flying home Wednesday. We and the boys are going through an "adjustment period." Sharon looks shell-shocked and has been muttering, "What have I done?" I have totally committed to victory and will not accept defeat. But we'll be fine (I'm into some nice Russian vodka). Talk to you soon.
> Rick and Sharon
>
> From: Rick
> To: Mike & Julia
> Subject: From Russia
> Date: Tuesday, September 11, 2007, at 02:10 AM
>
> Mike and Julia,
> One more day in Moscow then the flight from hell. The boys, believe it or not, seem to be responding (to a barely recognizable degree) to my efforts at parenting. Or perhaps my survival

instincts for self-deception have kicked in. Either way we may all live through this trip.

Rick and Sharon

Wednesday, we fly home.

One or both of us, have been awake with Hunter and Dylan for the last eight days, round the clock. We are mentally bankrupt and not thinking entirely clearly. To simplify things, I pay extra for VIP departure out of Moscow Sheremetyevo Airport, which allows us to sneak through a hidden door within the terminal and down a veiled hallway into the VIP room—bypassing the check-in and security lines—where we dawdle away four hours, during which the boys are restless and cranky and don't come close to controlling their bladders. Rick too, has come down with an unwelcome case of diarrhea, what we now refer to as "Russian flu."

Once aboard the airplane the kids begin screaming and don't stop for about an hour, during which their bowels are no more effective than a badly broken pipe. Every fifteen minutes, Rick's pipes make ugly noises and he shuffles to the bathroom.

Except for shrieking, pooping babies and a husband with his own bowel dilemmas and who loses color in his face and goes several shades of gray somewhere over the Atlantic, the flight is long but uneventful.

At some point a woman sitting two seats over notices Dylan in my lap and speaks to him in Russian. He doesn't respond until she tells him to point to her nose. Which he does. For the last eight days, my dear Dylan hasn't given me one smidgen of recognition, not a single gesture to let me know that he understands language, Russian or English, yet here he is listening and pointing away.

"Show me my nose," the woman says in Russian.

Dylan points to her nose.

"Show me my ear."

He reaches across me pointing at the woman's ear.

My boy is a genius, I just know it.

Chapter Twenty-Three

Home

·················

As we approach New York from the sky, Rick and I are physically and emotionally spent, exhausted in ways that don't register. What keeps us going is our boys, our need to band together, to shelter from harm, to champion a cause bigger than ourselves. Our need to love. We touch down and hustle off the plane. We visit the bathrooms and I change my one thousandth diaper. I navigate Hunter back into his frontpack and find Rick out on the concourse and pause to take a breath. I feel good. I lower my head and press it against Hunter's cheek. I could swear I feel his heartbeat, and I whisper to him. "This airport, it's the busiest in the world."

"Hartsfield Atlanta is busy," Rick says, conceivably thinking that I'm talking to him. He doesn't look at me but gazes forward, his neck strained, reading overhead signs and absently rocking little Dylan in front of him. "London Heathrow is busy."

"It doesn't matter," I murmur to Hunter.

My husband reveres facts, believes that facts are the raw material of meaning and to get the facts wrong is to destroy the meaning, or distort it. To raise a son (or two or three or four) with a distorted take on the meaning of things, well, that's not being a very good father now is it? Not if you can avoid it. Family is important to Rick this second go round. It was important the first go round but somehow things went awry. He hasn't said as much, but he's determined to be a better father and a small part of that bettering process is getting the facts straight from the get-go.

Me, I couldn't give two hoots about facts. That's not my job. My job is to woo my boys, to love them and explain things the way mothers do. I nudge Hunter higher in his frontpack so he can see what's what. I turn my body away so Rick doesn't hear (we are practically back to back), and I whisper to Hunter describing the colossal and, to a child at least, wondrous surroundings of JFK International. I point out the exposed steel structure and polished aluminum and all that glass, absorbing reflections and throwing them back at us in ways that make the glass look a foot thick.

"O'Hare International," Rick says. "Very busy."

"One hundred and fifty one gates," I whisper to Hunter. "I think that's right. Imagine finding your way with a few thousand vacationers in your path. Old ladies from Florida," and here I do an impression of an old lady who doesn't sound remotely from Florida, more like Mary Poppins, "and men with British accents, or Australian." I bend my head low enough to kiss Hunter on the head. I touch my lips to the skin of his scalp. It's like kissing a layer of soft parchment. My lips still pressed to his little coconut, I whisper, "Take your time. That's my advice. You'll be a word traveler someday, you and your brother, you'll see."

Hunter looks up at me with those big eyes, watching me, listening, and I want him to keep listening and not be startled by the chaotic surroundings. The key is to keep talking. I tell Hunter the airport was named after John F. Kennedy, the thirty-fifth president. A good man who was shot by a crazy person in 1963 who crouched in a window of a Dallas book depository and fired three shots and who two days later was shot by another crazy person. I run out of interesting airport trivia. "We better get a move on," Rick says.

We zig and zag our way to customs. This is the moment of truth, the fraction of a second when all the hard work and struggle to keep it together counts. At the customs counter the agent examines our passports, two American passports and two Russian. He looks past me to the scads of bodies queuing up. He says, "You have two new visitors with you, I see."

"My sons," I say. "Our sons."

He leans forward and places a little magnifying glass atop one of the passports. Without looking up, he says, "Mrs. Simons, can I ask you and your family to wait just over there?" He points to a door behind him and to the left.

"And what about these?" Rick says holding up the sealed brown envelopes.

"That's the place for those, too," he says.

We reach the door and Rick goes first. Beyond the door is a high counter and beyond that a man. I place passports on the counter and Rick adds the other paperwork. He puts the two brown envelopes on top of the pile. The man lifts the envelopes, shakes the packets and looks adoringly at Hunter and then at Dylan. "Thank you, Mr. Simons," he says. "Have a nice day."

"That's it?" Rick says.

"I can stretch it out; make you stand over there behind that line if you like?"

Rick bends ever so slightly at the waist, as if he might be feeling a touch of the Russian flu deep in his gut. No one speaks. We are momentarily stunned and in shock.

We move along winding our way to baggage claim past jillions of bodies in motion—old men moving at statue speeds and women in cushy eco-friendly shoes and business men in wrinkled Brooks Brothers suits and a few post-college backpackers returning from a world adventure they will brag about for the next four decades. We stand next to a baggage carousel.

Without asking I unsnap a buckle on Rick's pack, helping him unhook from Dylan so he can gallop to the toilet on a moment's notice. Hunter is now asleep, and I push his little head to one side of my frontpack, I move slowly trying not to wake him. I find it deeply agreeable to stand here with my husband and Hunter and Dylan, to stand here with my family.

Rick and I stand and frown at each other and try to make sense of our grand arrival.

"It seems too easy," I say.

"Compared to what?" he asks but he knows.

"What we've been through."

"If it's not hard, it's not real, is that it?" Rick says in a soft voice. "You think we need a final hurdle to jump over or, I don't know, one final immigration stamp?" He's stressed, partly sick, and completely exhausted from the culmination of travel, paperwork, and emotions. This is the end of our trip, the end of our magnificent adventure, an adventure we'll remember and talk about for the rest of our lives. Rick says, "What did you think? Did you expect to be fingerprinted?" The words are slightly argumentative, but the voice is genuinely caring and inquisitive, like a seasoned counselor.

"No."

"Photographed?"

"I'd settle for a gold star," I say.

"Me, too." He stares off into the distance. "Wait here. I'll be right back." With Dylan in tow, he marches back to the door and the high counter and the man standing there behind it. "Excuse me," Rick says. "I was just here. With two little boys, Russians. Isn't there any paperwork? A receipt, something?"

"You'll receive American paperwork in the mail," he says.

"That's it? We're official?"

"I'd give it sixty days," the man says.

"But we're official. My boys, my sons, my wife and I?"

"Your sons were citizens the moment they landed on U.S. soil."

"Okay then."

"Welcome home," the man says.

A buzzer sounds. The baggage carousel makes loud mechanical noises. The black rubbery part on top begins to move. We grab our luggage and take the shuttle to our car. The drive back to Delaware takes almost forever. We move on autopilot, too exhausted to think of much but making it home. Despite the fatigue, or maybe because of it, my mind begins to wander. Back to my father's childhood, my childhood, my traveling twenties, my first marriage, my up and down and ultimately empty prior relationships. My twisting path. I think of my love affair with Rick, and my harrowing, almost catastrophic attempts to conceive. Our hardships, the decisions, the uncertainties. Our journey.

We make it home. We do. My parents are waiting for us, eager to help.

To me, Rick asks, "How are you feeling?"

"You know the answer to that."

"Happy, your dream fulfilled," he says.

"This is what I've wanted my entire life." Holding my boys, I finally understand my journey. "What I wanted, what I am, is to be a mom."

That's what I am now and that's what I'll always be.

A mom at last.

Epilogue

······················

November 5, 2007

Dear Sharon,

In the middle of my busy day, I had a few thoughts I needed to say. But there are no words I can rhyme that can compare with those two little poems bouncing around our home. Their babbling and squeals are our poetry. Their playing together our movie. Their growth our joy. You have made this happen. Thank you, you wonderful Mom. So on your birthday this year, take time to reflect on our journey and the happiness we've made together.

Your loving husband,

Rick

Mother's Day, 2008

To Mommy (written by Dad) on your first Mother's Day:

We were trapped in Siberia hungry and cold

Dreaming of a mother courageous and bold

We had barely enough food, clothing and such,

But what we really needed was a mother's touch

You came and saved us with loving care,
And made us a home in Delaware.
While words can never express our thanks,
You'll have a clue,
By our joyful faces when we say
"Mommy we love you."
Dylan & Hunter

For news, information, and up-to-date photos of Dylan Dimitry Simons, Hunter Sergey Simons, and the rest of the family visit:

www.MomAtLast.com.

Sharon has also created the Adoption App visit:

www.theadoptionapp.com

Printed in the USA
CPSIA information can be obtained
at www.ICGtesting.com
JSHW022326140824
68134JS00019B/1318

9 781614 484424